THE END OF AMERICA

LETTER OF WARNING TO A YOUNG PATRIOT

NAOMI WOLF

CHELSEA GREEN PUBLISHING
WHITE RIVER JUNCTION, VERMONT

Developmental Editor: John Barstow
Editorial Director: Shay Totten
Project Manager: Emily Foote
Copy Editor: Nancy Crompton
Fact-checker: Mary Fratini
Book Designer: Peter Holm

Printed in Canada on recycled paper.
First printing, July 2007

10 9 8 7 6 5 4 3 2 1

Library of Congress Cataloging-in-Publication Data

Wolf, Naomi.
The end of America : a letter of warning to a young patriot / Naomi Wolf.
p. cm.
Includes bibliographical references.
ISBN 978-1-933392-79-0
1. Civil rights—United States. 2. Abuse of administrative power—United States. 3. National security—United States. 4. United States—Politics and government—2001- I. Title.

JC599.U5W63 2007
323.4'90973—dc22

2007024640

Chelsea Green Publishing Company
Post Office Box 428
White River Junction, VT 05001
(802) 295-6300
www.chelseagreen.com

For Arnold Hyman and Wende Jager Hyman
and for Chris and Jennifer Gandin Le,
who love this nation.

As nightfall does not come all at once, neither does oppression. In both instances, there is a twilight when everything remains seemingly unchanged. And it is in such a twilight that we all must be most aware of change in the air—however slight—lest we become unwitting victims of the darkness.

JUSTICE WILLIAM O. DOUGLAS

CONTENTS

We began with freedom.

Ralph Waldo Emerson

PREFACE

I wrote this book because I could no longer ignore the echoes between events in the past and forces at work today.

When I discussed these issues informally with a good friend who is the daughter of Holocaust survivors—and who teaches students about the American system of government as a kind of personal response to what happened to her family—she insisted that I present this argument.

I also wrote it as I did because, in the midst of my research, I went to Christopher Le and Jennifer Gandin's wedding.

Jennifer is one of our graduates—a gifted young writer who is the daughter of a Texas minister. Her American heartland roots reach back generations.

Chris—the "young patriot" of the subtitle—is a born activist, a natural grassroots leader and teacher. He helps run the National Suicide Prevention Lifeline and is active on a range of issues. They are characteristic of the kinds of the idealistic young people—idealistic *Americans*—who need to lead our nation out of this crisis.

I attended Chris and Jennifer's wedding on a warm day in early autumn. It was a scene of perfect Americana: the best of this nation's freedom, bounty, and shelter.

The celebration took place on a green slope along the Hudson River Valley. Jennifer's family decorated the ceremony and reception sites in billowing white chiffon; Chris's mother and his female relatives cooked for days to create wonderful Vietnamese dishes. Jennifer appeared for the vows themselves, glowing, in a white *ao dai,* the traditional Vietnamese wedding gown, then changed for the dancing—appearing equally radiant—into a purple American ball gown. There were children playing, trees soughing in the wind, the sun dappling the scene; there were toasts and gifts, a great DJ, and bad jokes. Friends of different races and backgrounds were dancing and chatting, and sharing in the affection we all had for the young couple. It was a scene of everything this country should be.

I was there having emerged from my reading and could not ignore the terrible storm clouds gathering in the nation at large, and I felt that the young couple needed one more gift: the tools to fully realize and defend their freedom; the means to be sure that their own children would be born in liberty.

This was not an academic thought. Chris's mother, Le Mai, who welcomed the guests with wit and style, is a heroine. She fled Vietnam as a young woman, a refugee—a "boat person"—with her less-than-two-months-old Vu (Chris's birth name) in her arms. She knew she had to risk her own life and her child's life for the chance to live in freedom.

With our own until-recent surfeit of liberty, we scarcely understand the preciousness of liberty as she does. But we have to reach this kind of understanding quickly, in order to contend with the crisis we face and to act with the urgency the time requires.

Chris and I have talked about liberty and his faith in the pendulum's ability to "swing back." He also believes many of his peers have little connection to democracy because previous generations have not brought it to life.

It is not just the young who are disconnected from democracy's tasks at just the moment that the nation's freedoms are being dismantled; in my travels across the country, I have heard from citizens of all backgrounds who feel alienated from the Founders' idea that *they* are the ones who must lead; *they* are the ones who must decide and confront and draw a line. They are the ones who matter. This book is written for them.

Such citizens need the keys to, the understanding of, the Founders' radical legacy. They need to understand how despots have gone about their work. They need a primer so they and those around them can be well-equipped for the fight that lies ahead.

So they can fight it well.
So that our children may continue to live in freedom.
So that we may all.

NAOMI WOLF
New York
June 24, 2007

— INTRODUCTION —

TEN STEPS

America was opened after the feudal mischief was spent. We began well. No inquisitions, here, no kings, no nobles…

RALPH WALDO EMERSON

Dear Chris:

I am writing because we have an emergency.

Here are U.S. news headlines from a two-week period in the late summer of 2006:

July 22: "CIA WORKER SAYS MESSAGE ON TORTURE GOT HER FIRED." Christine Axsmith, a computer security expert working for the C.I.A., said she had been fired for posting a message on a blog site on a top-secret computer network. Axsmith criticized waterboarding: "Waterboarding is torture, and torture is wrong." Ms. Axsmith lost her job as well as her top-secret clearance, which she had held since 1993. She fears her career in intelligence is over.[1]

July 28: "DRAFT BILL WAIVES DUE PROCESS FOR ENEMY COMBATANTS." The Bush administration has been working in secret on a draft bill "detailing procedures [for] bringing to trial those it captures in the war on terrorism, including some stark diversions from regular trial procedures. . . . Speedy trials are not required. . . . Hearsay information is admissible . . . the [military] lawyer can close the proceedings [and] can also order 'exclusion of the defendant' and his civilian counsel." Those defined as "enemy combatants" and "persons who have engaged in unlawful belligerence" can be held in prison until "the cessation of hostilities," no matter when that may be or what jail sentence they may get.[2]

July 29: "THE COURT UNDER SIEGE." In June 2006, the Supreme Court ruled that denying prisoners at Guantánamo judicial safeguards violated the Geneva Conventions and U.S. law. The Supreme Court also insisted that a prisoner be able to be present at his own trial. In response, the White House prepared a bill that "simply revokes that right." *The New York Times* editorial page warned, "It is especially frightening to see the administration use the debates over the prisoners at Guantánamo Bay and domestic spying to mount a new offensive against the courts."[3]

July 31: "A SLIP OF THE PEN." U.S. lawyers issued a statement expressing alarm at the way the president was overusing "signing statements." They argued that this was an exertion of executive power that undermined the Constitution. Said the head of the American Bar Association, "The threat to our Republic posed by presidential signing statements is both imminent and real unless immediate corrective action is taken."[4]

August 2: "BLOGGER JAILED AFTER DEFYING COURT ORDERS." A freelance blogger, Josh Wolf, 24, was jailed after he refused to turn over to investigators a video he had taken of a protest in San Francisco. Jane Kirtley, a professor of media ethics and law at the University of Minnesota, said that, although the jailing of American journalists was becoming more frequent, Mr. Wolf was the first American blogger she knew of to be imprisoned by federal authorities.[5]

August 2: "GOVERNMENT WINS ACCESS TO REPORTER PHONE RECORDS." "A federal prosecutor may inspect the telephone records of two *New York Times* reporters in an effort to identify their confidential sources. . ." according to *The New York Times*. A dissenting judge speculated that in the future, reporters would have to meet their sources illicitly, like drug dealers meeting contacts "in darkened doorways."[6]

August 3: "STRONG-ARMING THE VOTE." In Alabama, a federal judge took away powers over the election process from a Democratic official, Secretary of State Worley, and handed them over to a Republican governor: "[P]arty politics certainly appears to have been a driving force," argued the *Times.* "The Justice Department's request to shift Ms. Worley's powers to Governor Riley is extraordinary." When Worley sought redress in a court overseen by a federal judge aligned with the Bush administration, she wasn't allowed her chosen lawyer. It was "a one-sided proceeding that felt a lot like a kangaroo court. . ." cautioned the newspaper. She lost.[7]

Why am I writing this warning to you right now, in 2007? After all, we have had a Congressional election giving control of the House and the Senate to Democrats. The new leaders are at work. Surely, Americans who have been worried about erosions of civil liberties, and the destruction of our system of checks and balances, can relax now: see, the system corrects itself. It is tempting to believe that the basic machinery of democracy still works fine and that any emergency threatening it has passed—or, worst case, can be corrected in the upcoming presidential election.

But the dangers are not gone; they are regrouping. In some ways they are rapidly gaining force. The big picture reveals that ten classic pressures—pressures that have been used in various times and places in the past to close down pluralistic societies—were set in motion by the Bush administration to close down our own open society. These pressures have never been put in place before in this way in this nation.

A breather is unearned; we can't simply relax now. The laws that drive these pressures are still on the books. The people who have a vested interest in a less open society may be in a moment of formal political regrouping; but their funds are just as massive as before, their strategic thinking unchanged, and their strategy now is to regroup so that next time their majority will be permanent.[8]

All of us—Republicans, Democrats, Independents, American citizens—have little time to repeal the laws and roll back the forces that can bring about the end of the American system we have inherited from the Founders—a system that has protected our freedom for over 200 years.

I have written this warning because our country—the democracy our young patriots expect to inherit—is in the process of being altered forever. History has a great deal to teach us about what is happening right now—what has happened since 2001 and what could well unfold after the 2008 election. But fewer and fewer of us have read much about the history of the mid-twentieth century—or about the ways the Founders set up our freedoms to save us from the kinds of tyranny they knew could emerge in the future. High school students, college students, recent graduates, activists from all walks of life, have a sense that something overwhelming has been going on. But they have lacked a primer to brief them on these themes and put the pieces together, so it is hard for them to know how urgent the situation is, let alone what they need to do.

Americans expect to have freedom around us just as we expect to have air to breathe, so we have only limited understanding of the furnaces of repression that the Founders knew intimately. Few of us spend much time thinking about how "the system" they put in place protects our liberties. We spend even less time, considering how dictators in the past have broken down democracies or quelled pro-democracy uprisings. We take our American liberty for granted the way we take our natural resources for granted, seeing both, rather casually, as being magically self-replenishing. We have not noticed how vulnerable either resource is until very late in the game, when systems start to falter. We have been slow to learn that liberty, like nature, demands a relationship with us in order for it to continue to sustain us.

Most of us have only a faint understanding of how societies open up or close down, become supportive of freedom or ruled by fear, because this is not the kind of history that we feel, or that our educational system believes, is important for us to know. Another reason for our vagueness about how liberty lives or dies is that we have tended lately to subcontract out the tasks of the patriot: to let the professionals—lawyers, scholars, activists, politicians—worry about understanding the Constitution and protecting our rights. We think that "they" should manage our rights, the way we hire a professional to do our taxes; "they" should run the government, create policy, worry about whether democracy is up and running. We're busy.

But the Founders did not mean for powerful men and women far away from the citizens—for people with their own agendas, or for a class of professionals—to perform the patriots' tasks, or to protect freedom. They meant for us to do it: you, me, the American who delivers your mail, the one who teaches your kids.

I am one of the citizens who needed to relearn these lessons. Though I studied civics, our system of government was taught to me, as it was to you, as a fairly boring explication of a three-part civil bureaucracy, not as the mechanism of a thrilling, radical, and totally unprecedented experiment in human self-determination. My teachers explained that our three-part system was set up with "checks and balances," so that no one branch of government could seize too much power. Not so exciting: this sounded like "checks and balances" in a bureaucratic turf war. Our teachers failed to explain to us that the power that the Founders restrained in each branch of government is not abstract: it is the power to strip you and me of personal liberty.

So I needed to go back and read, more deeply than I had the first time around, histories of how patriots gave us our America out of the crucible of tyrants, as well as histories of how dictators came to power in the last century. I had to reread the stories of the making and the unmaking of freedom. The more I read these histories, the more disturbed I became.

I give you the lessons we can learn from them in this pamphlet form because of the crisis we face.

Like every American, I watched the events of September 11, 2001, with horror. Then, like many, I watched the reactions of the administration in power at first with concern, then with anxiety, and then, occasionally, with shock. I started feeling that there was something familiar about how events, at times, were unfolding.

Because of the déjà vu I was starting to feel when I read the newspaper every day, I began to take a second look at how leaders in the past had cracked down on societies over which they had gained control; I looked with special attention at what had happened when a leader brought about a shift from a pluralistic, democratic society to a dictatorship.

Historical Echoes

I began to think of these examples as "historical echoes"—not *proof* that someone influential in the administration had studied the details of mid-twentieth-century fascism and totalitarianism, but certainly suggestive.

What was it about the image of a mob of young men dressed in identical shirts, shouting at poll workers outside of a voting center in Florida during the 2000 recount, that looked familiar?[9] What resonated about the reports that Bush supporters in the South were holdings organized public events to burn CDs by the Dixie Chicks?[10] (CDs are actually quite hard to burn, and produce toxic fumes.) What seemed so familiar about an organized ideological group shaming an academic for saying something unpopular—and then pressuring the state government to get the university president to fire that professor?[11] What was so recognizable about reports that FBI agents were stopping peace activists at airports?[12] Why did the notion of being "greeted as liberators"[13] feel so familiar, and phrases such as "hiding in spider-holes"[14] sound so familiar?

These events may *seem* to have historical echoes because they actually *are* mirrored in history.

No one can deny the skill of fascists at forming public opinion. I can't prove that anyone in the Bush administration studied Joseph Goebbels. I am not trying to. All I am doing is noting echoes.

As you read you may notice other parallels—usually in the details of events. The Bush administration created a policy post-9/11 about liquids and air travel. Increased security restrictions led to airport security guards forcing some passengers to ingest liquids: A Long Island mother, for instance, was forced to drink from three bottles filled with her own breast milk prior to boarding a plane at JFK.[15] Other adult passengers have been forced to drink baby formula. In Benito Mussolini's era, one intimidation tactic was to force citizens to drink emetics and other liquids.[16] German SS men picked this up: they forced Wilhelm Sollmann, a Social Democrat leader, for instance, to drink castor oil and urine.[17] Of course baby formula is not an emetic. But a state agent—some agents are armed—forcing a citizen to ingest a liquid is a new scene in America.

In 2002 the Bush administration created and named the "Department of Homeland Security." White House spokespeople started to refer to the United States, unprecedentedly, as "the Homeland."[18] American Presidents have before now referred to the United States as "the nation" or "the Republic," and to the nation's internal policies as "domestic."

By 1930 Nazi propagandists referred to Germany not as "the nation" or "the Republic"—which it was—but rather as "the *Heimat*"—"the Homeland." *Homeland* is a word that memoirist Ernestine Bradley, who grew up in Nazi Germany, describes as saturated with nationalist power: "*Heimat* is a German word which has no satisfactory equivalent in other languages. It denotes the region where one has been born and remains rooted. . . . Longing to be in the *Heimat* causes the incurable disease of *Heimweh*."[19] Deputy Fuhrer Rudolf Hess, introducing Hitler at a Nuremberg rally, said, "Thanks to your leadership, Germany will be attainable as the Homeland—Homeland for all Germans in the world."[20] A Department of Domestic Security is simply a bureaucracy, capable of mistakes; a department protecting our "Homeland" has a different authority.

In 2001 the USA PATRIOT Act let the federal government compel doctors to give up confidential medical records without a warrant demonstrating probable cause. Your previously private interaction with your doctor is now subject to state scrutiny.[21] (Nazi law in the 1930s required German doctors to disclose citizens' previously private medical records to the State.)

In 2005 *Newsweek* reported that Guantánamo prisoners had seen the Koran being flushed down toilets. Under pressure from the White House, the magazine ran a correction: It had not interviewed direct witnesses to the practice.[22] But human rights organizations did confirm accounts of similar abuses of the Koran.[23] (In 1938, the Gestapo forced Jews to scrub out the toilets with their sacred phylacteries, the *tfillin*.)[24]

Amnesty International reports that U.S. interrogators torment prisoners in Iraq by playing heavy metal at top volume into their cells night and day.[25] (In 1938, the Gestapo tormented imprisoned Austrian premier Kurt von Schuschnigg by keeping the radio on at top volume, night and day.)[26]

An Iraqi human rights group complained that, in 2004, U.S. forces seized the innocent wives of suspected insurgents and held the women hostage in order to pressure their husbands to turn themselves in.[27] (In Joseph Stalin's Russia, secret police took hostage the innocent wives of dissidents accused of "treason," to pressure their husbands to turn themselves in.)[28]

When the United States invaded Iraq, Vice President Dick Cheney promised that we would be "greeted as liberators." (When the German army occupied the Rhineland, Nazi propaganda asserted that the troops would be welcomed as liberators.)

President Bush argued that the prisoners in Guantánamo Bay could be treated harshly because they were not covered by the Geneva Conventions. (Nazis asserted that the troops invading Russia should treat the enemy especially brutally, because they were not covered by the Hague Conventions.)[29]

After 9/11, then–National Security Advisor Condoleezza Rice

and Vice President Cheney coined a new phrase: America was now on a "war footing."[30] Superficially, it was a stirring word choice. But if you thought about it, it was also kind of an *odd* word choice, because America was not actually at war. What *is* a "war footing"? (Nazi leaders explained, after the Reichstag fire, that Germany, which was not actually at war, was from then on a permanent "*kriegsfusz*"—literally, a "war footing.")

The Bush White House "embedded" reporters with U.S. military units in Iraq. Uncritical coverage of the war expanded considerably. (National Socialist propaganda officials embedded reporters and camera crews with their own armed forces: Filmmaker Leni Riefenstahl was embedded with Nazi troops in Poland;[31] U.S. correspondent William Shirer drove with German units into occupied France.)[32]

The Bush administration unloads coffins of dead American soldiers from planes at night and has forbidden photographers to take pictures of the coffins.[33] (National Socialists unloaded the coffins of the German war dead at night.)

The White House announced, beginning in 2002, that there were terrorist "sleeper cells" scattered throughout the nation. A "sleeper cell," press reports explained, was a group of terrorists that had merged into ordinary American life, waiting, perhaps for years, for the signal to rise up and cause mayhem.

A wave of reporting asserted that the FBI had located a sleeper cell in Lodi, California. After an informant had been paid hundreds of thousands of dollars to spy on Muslims, the FBI detained a Muslim father and son, Umer Hayat, and his son, Hamid Hayat.[34] The two men explained that they had confirmed an imaginary sleeper cell in order to end a terrifying series of interrogations.[35]

Another much-publicized sleeper cell identified four Muslim men in Detroit. Attorney General John Ashcroft claimed that the men had had advance knowledge of 9/11;[36] federal authorities charged that they were part of a "sleeper cell plotting attacks against Americans overseas," as news reports put it.[37] The Justice

Department heralded the arrests as one of its biggest hits in the War on Terror.

The phrase "sleeper cell" entered deeply into the American unconscious, even becoming the plot of a 2005 TV movie. But in 2006, Richard Convertino, the prosecutor of the Detroit case, was indicted on charges of trying to present false evidence at the trial, and concealing other evidence, in his attempt to back up the government's theory about the men. All charges were dropped against the men and the Justice Department quietly repudiated its own case.[38] But you probably didn't hear about that, and the creepy sleeper-cell narrative stayed in the atmosphere to trouble your dreams.

Sleeper cell was a term most Americans had never heard before. It is a phrase from Stalin's Russia, where propagandists said that imaginary cells, consisting of agents of "international capitalism"—that is, us—had been sent by the U.S. government to infiltrate Soviet society. These secret agents would pose as good Soviet comrades, living quietly among their neighbors, but just awaiting the day when, at a signal, they would all rise up to commit mayhem.[39]

When the 2006 terrorist plot against U.S.-bound planes was uncovered in London, an FBI official gave a much-quoted sound bite: "If this plot had actually occurred, the world would have stood still."[40] FBI guys don't usually speak in cadences of dark poetry. (Of his plans in 1940, Hitler said, "The world will hold its breath.")[41]

These echoes are worth noticing—but are not ultimately that important. What *is* important are the structural echoes you will see: the way dictators take over democracies or crush pro-democracy uprisings by invoking emergency decrees to close down civil liberties; creating military tribunals; and criminalizing dissent.

Those echoes are important.

So I read about Mussolini's Italy in the 1920s; Stalin's Russia and Hitler's Germany in the 1930s; I read about East Germany in the

1950s and Czechoslovakia in the 1960s and Chile in 1973, as well as about other Latin American dictatorships; I read about Communist China in the late 1980s and early 1990s.

The countries I looked at were very different, of course, and the violent dictators had a broad range of ideologies. Stalin imposed totalitarianism over a communist state, itself built upon the ruins of a toppled monarchy. Mussolini and Hitler both came to power legally in the context of fragile parliamentary democracies. East Germany and Czechoslovakia were communist systems and China still is; and General Augusto Pinochet closed down Chile's young democracy in a classic Latin American military coup d'état.

Violent dictators across the political spectrum all do the same key things. Control is control. In spite of this range of ideological differences, profound similarities in tactics leap off the pages. Each of these leaders used, and other violent dictators around the globe continue to borrow, the same moves to close down open societies or crush dissent.

There are ten steps that are taken in order to close down a democracy or crush a prodemocratic movement, whether by capitalists, communists, or right-wing fascists. These ten steps, together, are more than the sum of their parts. Once all ten have been put in place, each magnifies the power of the others and of the whole.

Impossible as it may seem, we are seeing each of these ten steps taking hold in the United States today.

But America is different! I can hear you saying.

There is no guarantee that America is different if Americans fail to take up the patriot's task.

At times in our own history our commitment to freedom has faltered. The Alien and Sedition Act of 1798 made it a crime for Americans to speak critically— to "bring into contempt or disrepute"—of then-President John Adams and other U.S. leaders. But Thomas Jefferson pardoned those convicted under these laws when he took office.

During the Civil War, President Lincoln suspended habeas corpus, effectively declaring martial law in several states: Close to 38,000 Americans were imprisoned by military authorities during the war—many for simply expressing their views. But when the war ended in 1865, the Supreme Court ruled that it had been unconstitutional for military tribunals to try civilians.

In 1918, labor leader Eugene Debs was arrested for giving a speech about the First Amendment; he got a ten-year jail sentence. Raids swept up hundreds of other activists.[42] But after World War I ended, the hysteria subsided.

During World War II, the Justice Department rounded up 110,000 innocent Japanese-Americans and imprisoned them in camps. When the war was over, these innocent Americans were released as well.

Anti-communist anxiety led the nation to tolerate the McCarthy hearings; but the pendulum swung back and Senator Joe McCarthy himself was condemned by his colleagues.

I am describing the movement of "the pendulum"—as in the American cliché, "The pendulum always swings back." We are so familiar with, and so reliant upon, the pendulum. That is why you are so sure that "America is different." But the pendulum's working depends on unrestricted motion. In America, up until now, the basic checks and balances established by the Founders have functioned so well that the pendulum has always managed to swing back. Its very success has made us lazy. We trust it too much, without looking at what a pendulum requires in order to function: the stable framework that allows movement; space in which to move; that is, liberty.

The pendulum cannot work now as it has before. There are now two major differences between these past examples of the pendulum's motion and the situation we face today.

First, as Bruce Fein of the American Freedom Agenda and writer Joe Conason have both noted, previous wars and emergencies have had endpoints. But President Bush has defined the current conflict with global terrorism as being open-ended. This is a permanent alteration of the constitutional landscape.

The other difference between these examples and today is that when prior dark times unfolded in America, we forbade torture, and the rule of law was intact. Legal torture, as you will see, acting in concert with the erosion of the rule of law, changes what is possible.

So, because I was looking at something unprecedented in our nation's history, I had to read the histories of many forms of state repression, including the most extreme.

I had to include Nazi Germany in my scrutiny of repressive governments. Many people are understandably emotionally overwhelmed when the term "Nazism" or the name "Hitler" is introduced into debate. As someone who lost relatives on both sides of my family in the Holocaust, I know this feeling. I also know that there is a kind of intellectual etiquette, an unwritten rule, that Nazism and Hitler should be treated as stand-alone categories.

But I believe this etiquette is actually keeping us from learning what we have to learn right now. I believe we honor the memory of the victims of Nazism with our willingness to face the lessons that history—even the most nightmarish history—can offer us about how to defend freedom.

In looking at other violent dictatorships, including Germany's, I am not comparing the United States in 2007 to Nazi Germany, or Bush to Hitler. The two nations and leaders inhabit different worlds. There will not be a coup in America like Mussolini's March on Rome or a dramatic massacre like Hitler's Night of the Long Knives. But certain threads are emerging that have connections to the past. I *am* calling your attention to important lessons from history about how fragile civil liberties are, and how quickly freedom can be lost. I ask you to quiet your understandable aversion long enough to walk with me through the material I have to show you.

The ten steps to dictatorship are basic.

In September 2006, military leaders staged a coup in Thailand, which had been a noisy democracy. In a matter of days, the coup leaders ticked through many of the ten steps, as if they had a shopping list. In a sense they did.

They deployed armed guards in residential neighborhoods, sent lawmakers home, shut down the free press, took over the state-run television, threatened critics with arrest, put new limits on travel, restricted protest, and discontinued the Parliamentary rule of law. Thailand was a police state within a matter of days.[43]

We are seeing each of the basic ten steps being put into place here in the United States today—more quietly, more gradually, and sometimes more elegantly; but each is underway.

My sense of alarm comes from the clear lessons from history that, once certain checks and balances are destroyed, and once certain institutions have been intimidated, the pressures that can turn an open society into a closed one turn into direct assaults; at that point events tend to occur very rapidly, and a point comes at which there is no easy turning back to the way it used to be.

The fascist shift does not progress like a diagonal line rising steadily across a chart. Rather, it progresses in a buildup of many acts assaulting democracy simultaneously, that then form a critical mass—what writer Malcolm Gladwell would call a "tipping point." The pressure from this set of assaults suddenly pushes the nation into a new and degraded reality. The turning points can be mapped as vertical lines—the point at which prisoners lost the right to habeas corpus, for instance, is one—which then plateau into the nation's new normal. The nation acclimates; then this process begins again at that greater level of suppression.

What got to be really scary in my reading was how predictable events become, once you are familiar with the blueprint. By the beginning of August, 2006, for instance, it seemed like a good bet that the Bush administration would soon move on from the detainee bill that it had been secretly preparing to seek Congressional authorization for creating a prison beyond the rule of law where torture could take place. This was accomplished by October of 2006.

In September of 2006, I thought that it was likely that some of the first prisoners to be tried in Guantánamo by the new military commission system would be white and English-speaking. Indeed, that happened by April of 2007. It also seemed probable that White House spokespeople would begin to use terms such as *treason*, *espionage*, *subversion*, and *aiding the enemy* to describe criticism, press scrutiny, dissent, and even simple departure from alignment with White House goals. From the blueprint, I thought it was unsurprising when the administration started to criminalize speech in new ways. This began to happen in earnest by May of 2007.

When the U.S. Attorney scandal came to light in March of 2007 and there was still little information, because I had been reading a biography of Goebbels, I remarked to a friend, "I bet the attorneys were in swing states." By the next week, it had been confirmed that most of them were in fact in swing states. All this supposition was not rocket science; it was simply that each of these is a classic move in the playbook of a fascist shift.

Everything changed in America in September of 2006, when Congress passed the Military Commissions Act.[44] This law created a new legal reality that heralds the end of America if we do not take action. Yet most Americans still do not understand what happened to them when that law passed.

This law gives the president—any president—the authority to establish a separate justice system for trying alien unlawful enemy combatants. It defines both "torture" and "materially support[ing] hostilities" broadly. The MCA justice system lacks the basic protections afforded defendants in our domestic system of laws, in our military justice system, or in the system of laws used to try war criminals—Nazi leaders got better civil liberty protection than alien enemy combatants, as did perpetrators of genocide like Slobodan Milosovic. And persons accused by the president (or his designees) of being alien unlawful enemy combatants are forbidden from invoking the Geneva Conventions, a treaty that represents the basic protections of justice common to all civilized nations. The United States has signed the Geneva Conventions and agreed to abide by them, and this repudiation is a radical departure from our traditions. Under the MCA, the government can used "coerced" interrogation to obtain evidence. Finally, and perhaps most damagingly, the MCA denies unlawful alien enemy combatants the right to challenge the legitimacy of their confinement or treatment. So, while the MCA provides all sorts of rules that the military is supposed to follow, it will be difficult, if not impossible to hold anyone accountable for breaking those rules.

But this is not all. The president and his lawyers now claim the authority to designate any American citizen he chooses as being an "enemy combatant"; and to define both "torture" and "material support" broadly. They claim the authority to give anyone in the executive branch the power to knock on your door, seize you on the street, or grab you as you are changing planes at Newark or Atlanta airports; blindfold you and put earphones on you; take you to a cell in a navy prison; keep you in complete isolation for months or even years; delay your trial again and again; and make it hard for you to communicate with your lawyer. The president claims the authority to direct agents to threaten you in interrogations and allow into your trial things you confessed to while you were being mistreated.

The president claims the authority to do any of those things to any American citizen now on his say-so alone. Let me repeat this: The president asserts that he can do this to you even if you have never committed a crime of any kind: "enemy combatant" is a status offense. Meaning that if the president says you are one, then you are.

Human rights groups raised the alarm early on about what this law might mean to the many innocent foreign detainees who had been swept up in the machinery of Afghan prisons and sent to Guantánamo. Some Congressional leaders have warned us about what this law might do to our own soldiers, if they are taken as POWs. But most ordinary citizens did not understand what

Congress had done—not to anonymous, possibly scary, brown people on a faraway island, but to them. Most Americans still do not understand.

Last September, concerned about the legal arguments being put forward by the Department of Justice, I called a friend who is a professor of Constitutional law.

"Does the administration assert that the president can define anyone he wants to as an 'enemy combatant'? Including U.S. citizens?" I asked.

"Yes," he replied.

"And does it argue that courts must defer to the government's assertions that someone should be held as an enemy combatant, even when it presents no direct evidence?"

"Yes," he replied.

"So doesn't that mean they are saying that now any of us for any reason he decides can be seized off the street and imprisoned in isolation for months and interrogated?"

"Yes," he said.

"So why isn't anyone saying that?"

"Some people are. But a lot of people probably think it would just sound crazy," he replied.[45]

— CHAPTER ONE —

The FOUNDERS *and the* FRAGILITY *of* DEMOCRACY

But a constitution of government, once changed from freedom, can never be restored. Liberty, once lost, is lost forever.

JOHN ADAMS,

letter to Abigail Adams, July 7, 1775

To U. S. citizens in the year 2007, the very title of this book should be absurd. It is unthinkable to most of us that there could ever be an "end of America" in the metaphorical sense. But it is when memories are faint about coercive tactics that worked to control people in the past that people can be more easily controlled in the present.

When I say that the Bush administration has used tactics that echo certain tactics from the past, I am making a conservative argument. You will have to look at the echoes I note and decide for yourself what to make of them. We know that Karl Rove seeks the goal of a permanent majority. A permanent majority is easier to solidify for the future if democracy's traditional challenges to power are weakened or silenced.

I won't insult Republicans by calling this goal a "permanent Republican majority," although Rove calls it by that name. Most Americans—Republican, Independent, or Democrat—are patriots and believe in the Founders' vision. I have to assume that one reason for this assault on democracy is to secure the "permanent majority" status of a far smaller group, or rather of several smaller groups, driven by motives of power and money: the great power represented by access to an executive that is driving an agenda unthreatened by the people's will, and the vast amount of money that has begun to flow from a condition of uninterrupted domestic surveillance and open-ended foreign hostilities.

Authoritarianism, Fascism, Totalitarianism: Some Definitions

Are any of these terms legitimate for this discussion?

I have made a deliberate choice in using the terms *fascist tactics* and *fascist shift* when I describe some events in America now. I stand by my choice. I am not being heated or even rhetorical; I am being technical.

Americans tend to see democracy and fascism as all-or-nothing categories. But it isn't the case that there is a pure, static "democracy" in the white squares of a chessboard and a pure, static "fascism" in the black squares. Rather, there is a range of authoritarian regimes, dictatorships, and varieties of Fascist state, just as there are stronger and weaker democracies—and waxing and waning democracies. There are many shades of gray on the spectrum from an open to a closed society.

Totalitarianism, of course, is the blackest state. Mussolini adopted the term *totalitarian* to describe his own regime.[1] Political philosopher Hannah Arendt writes of the post–World War I era and the "undermining of parliamentary government," succeeded by "all sorts of new tyrannies, Fascist and semi-Fascist, one-party and military dictatorships," and culminating at last in "the seemingly firm establishment of totalitarian governments resting on mass support" in Russia and in Germany.

Arendt sees Germany and Italy as variations on the same model of totalitarianism. She defines *totalitarianism* as a mass movement with a leadership that requires "total domination of the individual." A totalitarian leader, in her view, faces no opposition—it has gone quiet—and he can unleash terror without himself being afraid.[2]

Fascism is a word whose definition political scientists (and even fascists themselves) do not entirely agree upon. Though Mussolini coined this term (from the dual rods, or *fasces*, carried by officials in ancient Rome), some Nazis did not see the Italians as being tough enough to qualify as true fascists. Umberto Eco wrote of latter-day "Ur-Fascists" and other critics have described "neo-Fascists" or "sub-fascists" when they refer to more recent violent dictatorships that use state terror and other kinds of control to subordinate the population and crush democratic impulses—notably in Latin America.[3] The *Columbia Encyclopedia* defines fascism as a "philosophy of government that glorifies the state and nation and assigns to the state control over every aspect of national life. . . . Its essentially vague and emotional nature facilitates the development of unique national varieties, whose leaders often deny indignantly that they are fascists at all."[4]

Throughout this letter of warning, I will use the term "a fascist shift." It is a wording that describes a process. Both Italian and German fascisms came to power legally and incrementally in functioning democracies; both used legislation, cultural pressure, and baseless imprisonment and torture, progressively to consolidate power. Both directed state terror to subordinate and control the individual, whether the individual supported the regime inwardly or not. Both were rabidly antidemocratic, not as a side sentiment but as the basis of their ideologies; and yet both aggressively used the law to pervert and subvert the law.

This process is what I mean when I refer to "fascist shift." Two aspects of most definitions of fascism are relevant here: *Fascist* refers to a militaristic system that is opposed to democracy and seeks, ideologically and practically, to crush it. And fascism uses state terror against the individual to do this. When I talk about a "fascist shift" in America, I am talking about an antidemocratic ideology that uses the threat of violence against the individual in order to subdue the institutions of civil society, so that they in turn can be subordinated to the power of the state.

This fascist shift has proven compact, effective, and exportable, long after these two regimes met their end in World War II. If it is too emotionally overwhelming to think of Italy and Germany, you can consider the more recent fates of Indonesia, Nicaragua, Chile, Uruguay, Paraguay, and Guatemala, all of which suffered widespread state terror and the activation of many of the ten steps that I describe, as leaders sought to subdue the people. A fascist shift brings about a violent dictatorship in a context where democracy could have taken the nation toward freedom.

Some critics responding to an essay I wrote laying out the spine of this argument were more comfortable with the term *authoritarian* than with *fascist*. A number of U.S. writers have used "authoritarian" to describe the Bush administration. Authoritarian, in contrast—the term Joe Conason uses, for example, in his prescient book *It Can Happen Here*—means that one branch of government has seized power from the others.[5] (The *Concise Oxford Dictionary* defines it as "favouring, encouraging, or enforcing strict obedience to authority, as opposed to individual freedom. . . .")[6] Conason's argument is entirely right for where we are at this point: in July of 2007, America actually already *has* an executive who is disregarding the restraints of the two other branches of government.

But authoritarianism has many guises, and some are relatively livable for most people. For instance, you can have a military leadership in an authoritarian system, but you can have fairly independent courts and a fairly independent press. Indeed, people can see authoritarianism as rather attractive in what they understand to be a time of national emergency. Authoritarianism can be downright cozy compared to some alternatives. The grave danger in America is that events are not stopping here.

When I refer to other societies, I use the terms *totalitarianism*, *fascism*, and *authoritarianism* where they are appropriate.

State terror directed against the individual is the difference between a fairly stable American authoritarianism and the fascist shift I am writing to you about. Theorists such as Arendt and

Zbigniew Brzezinski saw top-down terror to be at the heart of both Nazi and Soviet regimes. They argue that it was the overwhelming power of the secret police agencies such as the Gestapo and the KGB that led to the fear that blanketed these societies.[7] More recent historians focus on how populations in fascist or totalitarian systems adapt to fear through complicity: In this view, when a minority of citizens is terrorized and persecuted, a majority live out fairly normal lives by stifling dissent within themselves and going along quietly with the state's acts of violent repression. The authors of an oral history of Nazi Germany point out that, though it may sound shocking, fascist regimes can be "quite popular" for the people who are not being terrorized.[8]

Both perspectives are relevant here: Top-down edicts generate fear, but when citizens turn a blind eye to state-sanctioned atrocities committed against others, so long as they believe themselves to be safe, a fascist reality has fertile ground in which to take root.

American Fascism?

When America gets fascism it will be called anti-fascism.

Attributed to Huey Long

America has flirted with fascism before. In the 1920s, a number of newspaper editors in the United States were impressed with the way that fascism coordinated with capitalism.[9] In the 1930s, when Americans were suffering from economic depression and labor unrest, some U.S. leaders looked at the apparent order that Mussolini and Hitler had imposed on their own previously chaotic, desperate nations, and wondered if a "strong man" approach would serve the nation better than our own battered system. As historian Myra MacPherson puts it, "In the thirties there was alarming support for Hitler [in America], with American-style brownshirts proliferating. . . ."[10] Nineteen-thirties American fascism boasted many followers, nationally known demagogues, and even its own celebrities, such as aviator Charles Lindbergh, one of the most famous Americans of the day.

Some commentators of the era speculated that demagogues might spearhead an extreme patriotic movement such as those in Italy and Germany. In 1935, crusading journalist I. F. Stone compared Huey Long's dismantling of democracy in Louisiana to Hitler's legislation dissolving local self-government.

In 1939 author James Wechsler wrote, "There was genuine fear that a fascist movement had finally taken root in New York," where reactionary hooligans were staging anti-Semitic street fights modeled on the German youth actions.[11] Other U.S. intellectuals thought the time was right to develop an American fascist mystique themselves, and began to do so.

American interest in fascism was prevalent enough for popular writer Sinclair Lewis to satirize it in his 1935 classic, *It Can't Happen Here*. Lewis, as Conason eloquently notes, showed step by step the ways in which it—a fascist coup—*could* theoretically "happen here." Though many mocked Sinclair's premise in 1935, many others read his fable of warning and thought more seriously about the dangers that American fascism really represented. It was healthy for Americans at that time to imagine the worst that could unfold if the nation chose to follow the seductions of fascism any further.

What Is Freedom?

"It's a free country," any American child will say, a comfortable assurance that this same American carries as he or she grows up. We scarcely consider that that sentence descends to that child from arguments for liberty that date back through generations of Enlightenment-era English and French philosophers, who were trying to work out what "a free country" could possibly look like—even as they themselves lived though or looked back on reigns of violently abusive and capricious monarchs.

We tend to think of American democracy as being somehow eternal, ever-renewable, and capable of withstanding all assaults. But the Founders would have thought we were dangerously naïve, not to mention lazy, in thinking of democracy in this way. This view—which we see as patriotic—is the very opposite of the view that they held. They would not have considered our attitude patriotic—or even American: The Founders thought, in contrast, that it was *tyranny* that was eternal, ever-renewable, and capable of withstanding all assaults, whereas *democracy* was difficult, personally exacting, and vanishingly fragile. The Founders did not see Americans as being special in any way: They saw America—that is, the process of liberty—as special.

In fact, the men who risked hanging to found our nation, and the women who risked their own lives to support this experiment in freedom, and who did what they could to advance it, were terrified of exactly what we call dictatorship. They called it "tyranny" or "despotism." It was the specter at their backs—and they all knew it—as Americans debated the Constitution and argued about the shape of the Bill of Rights.

The framing of the documents upon which the new national government rested did not take place as we were taught it did—in a sunny glow of confident assertiveness about freedom. That scenario is a Hallmark-card rewrite of the real mood of the era and the tenor that surrounded the discussions of the day. The mood as early Americans debated the proposed Constitution and the Bill of Rights was, rather, one of grave apprehension.

For the Founders shared with the rest of the people awaiting the outcome of their labors a dread of what nearly all of them—Federalist or anti-Federalist—saw as the real prospect of a tyrannical force rising up in America. This repressive force could take many forms: the form of a rapacious Congress oppressing the people; the form of an out-of-control executive; or even the form of the people themselves, cruelly oppressing a minority.[12] The Constitution and the Bill of Rights were set forth not as a flag flying merrily but as a bulwark: a set of barriers against what the Founders and their fellow countrymen and women saw as people's natural tendency to oppress others if their power is unchecked.

What recurred regularly in various arguments as the Constitution and the Bill of Rights took shape was the widespread fear of an unchecked executive.[13] It's not surprising that these patriots would so deeply fear a single man invested with too much power. They had just freed themselves from being subjugated to George III, an abusive, not to mention mentally ill, monarch.

The Founders had fled repressive societies themselves, or were children or grandchildren of those who had done so. The North American colonies were settled by people—Puritans, Quakers and others—who had fled countries in which they had been imprisoned and even tortured for such acts as assembling in groups to pray; or for attending certain churches; or for publishing pamphlets critical of the King or of Parliament. The Founders knew from their own experience how the Crown treated those who talked about democracy (that is, "sedition"). They knew about criminalized speech, arbitrary arrest, and even show trials. They had personally to reckon with the risk of state-sanctioned torture and murder: Each of the men who signed the Declaration of Independence could have been hanged if the colonies had lost the Revolutionary War.

When Thomas Paine wrote *Common Sense*, the little book that helped start the big revolution, he risked being hanged by the British Crown for treason. Indeed, the Crown did charge Paine with sedition for having written another book, *The Rights of Man*. He was tried by a jury hand-chosen by the government that he had attacked—a jury sure to condemn him. The proceedings were a mockery of the rule of law. In spite of his lawyer's brilliant defense, as one witness put it, "the venal jury . . . without waiting for any answer, or any summing up by the Judge, pronounced [Paine] guilty. Such an instance of infernal corruption is scarcely upon record." Paine's publisher was dragged off to prison in chains.[14]

Arbitrary arrest, state intimidation, and torture were the tactics of the tyrannical monarchs of eighteenth century Europe—tactics that the Founders sought to banish from American soil forever. The Founders' rebellion on this continent intended systematically to open a nation up to freedom—meaning, fundamentally, freedom from these evils.

In colleges with progressive curricula, the Founders are often portrayed as "dead white men," whose vision was imperfect, who denied women and the poor civil rights, and who defined an African slave in America as being three-fifths of a person; old guys in wigs who wrote documents that are now dusty in language that seems to us to be either arcane or to offer sentiments that are so obvious now they have become clichés (". . . life, liberty, and the pursuit of happiness. . .").

Here's what we're not taught: Those words at the time they were written were blazingly, electrifyingly subversive. If you understand them truly now, they still are. These men and the women who supported their work were walking further out into the unknown—betting on ordinary people's capacities—than anyone had ever walked in the history of the human race. You are not taught—and it is a disgrace that you aren't—that these men and women were radicals for liberty; that they had a vision of equality that was a slap in the face of what the rest of their world understood to be the unchanging, God-given order of nations; and that they were willing to die to make that desperate vision into a reality for people like us, whom they would never live to see.

You weren't taught that the way they brought the freest nation in the world into being was by reading passionately about fledgling democracies of the past; by positioning their imaginations directly against the violent repressions they had fled; and by carefully, delicately crafting a mechanism of checks and balances, and a bill of rights, that would protect these extreme manifestations of freedom. The Founders set out to prove that ordinary people could be entrusted with governing themselves in a state where no one could arbitrarily arrest them, lock them up, or torture them.

Living against the backdrop of violent repression, these men and women saw the democracy they were seeking to establish, and the checks and balances that protected it, as being in need of continual rededication against potential tyrants *in America* who would want to subjugate *Americans*.

Thomas Jefferson's initial reaction to the proposed Constitution was negative, for, as he wrote to James Madison, he feared the possibility of the rise of an American tyrant: ". . . Roman emperors, popes, German emperors, deys of the Ottoman dependencies, and Polish kings—all were elective in some sense." Indeed, historian Bernard Bailyn sees that "[T]he fear of power—the very heart of the original Revolutionary ideology—was an animating spirit behind all of [Jefferson's] thinking. . . ."[15]

Jefferson wasn't alone in the Revolutionary generation in fearing an American despot. After the publication of the proposed Constitution in 1787, critics shared his apprehension. They feared a president's treaty-making power, because they were worried he might make deals in secret. They worried about his power to make certain decisions without a two-thirds majority, because they feared he might do anything he wanted with that power. They argued that an American executive would not be immune to despotic temptations, just as an unchecked Congress would not be immune.[16]

The authors of *The Federalist Papers*—Alexander Hamilton, James Madison, and John Jay—wrote that series of essays to help reassure their fellow Americans. They did so by explaining that the complex web of tensions they were proposing—these "checks and balances"—would prevent a person or a group united in "a common interest or passion" from depriving others of their rights. Hamilton, Madison, and Jay did not think that this web was self-sustaining. They thought that the delicate mechanism of the interdependent executive, legislative, and judiciary branches was only as reliable as the character of the people who were either protecting or abandoning it. They saw all people as corruptible and so set up the system to keep *anyone* from having unconfined power.[17]

It was a truism to the Revolutionary generation that if the fragile mechanism became unbalanced, American leaders too—*of course*—would revert to brutality. We are so removed from the tyranny that the nation's first patriots experienced personally that we have not only forgotten this crucial insight, we have even forgotten to consider how obvious it was to the fathers and mothers of our country.

The Founders never expected us to fall asleep or get lazy. They counted on us to keep the web of the precious system intact so that an American despot could never arise. They trusted us to cherish liberty as they did.

The price of liberty, the generation that debated and created the Constitution understood, is eternal vigilance.

The Strength and Ease of Dictatorship

There is also a reverse process that systematically closes down freedom.

Many Americans have an impressionistic sense that Mussolini and Hitler came to power through violence alone. But each came to power legally in a working democracy; each made use of the Parliamentary system itself to subvert and reorder the rule of law; and each then, quickly, *legally* aggregated state power overwhelmingly in his own person. Both leaders were supported by sophisticated intellectuals and political theorists who made the case to the people that democratic processes weakened the nation in a time of crisis.

All dictators: invoke an external and threat; develop a paramilitary force; create a secret prison system; surveil ordinary citizens; arbitrarily detain and release them; harass citizens' groups; target writers, entertainers, and other key individuals for dissenting; intimidate the press; recast dissent as "treason" and criticism as "espionage"; and eventually subvert the rule of law.

Unfortunately, while it is very difficult to sustain an open society, history shows that it is fairly simple to close one down.

The same ten steps have shut down democracies all over the world at many different times. And these steps are no secret: After all, Mussolini studied Lenin;[18] Hitler studied Mussolini;[19] Stalin studied Hitler;[20] and Chinese communist leaders studied Stalin, and so on. Indeed the United States has helped develop a training center, the School of the Americas (now renamed the Western Hemisphere Institute for Security Cooperation), to train various procapitalist Latin American leaders in the theory and practice of violent dictatorship.[21]

Is the United States in 2007 parallel to Italy in 1922 or Germany in 1933, Czechoslovakia in 1968, Chile in 1973, or China in 1989? No. But over the past six years we have been watching the United States move closer to becoming a more closed society.

The Appearance of Normalcy in an Early Fascist Shift

It's easy to look around at America in 2007 and choose to believe that this warning is overheated: After all, we are for the most part doing what we have routinely done. We are going online into a vibrant Internet world; clicking through hundreds of TV channels; enjoying Hollywood films; reading bestsellers that present views across the political spectrum. The courts are ruling, newspapers are publishing exposés, protest marches are being planned about the war; a presidential race is underway.

But there are plenty of examples of a shift into a dictatorial reality in which, for several years, while the basic institutions of freedom are targeted and rights are eroding, daily life still looks very normal—even, for many people, pleasant.

Americans tend to think of the shift to fascism in scary set-pieces: the boots on the stairs, the knock in the middle of the night, the marching columns, the massive banners waving over city streets; a Leni Riefenstahl film all the time, or an unrelieved scene of citizen terror with crematoria smoking in the distance. We are so used to seeing depictions of the most sensational aspects of totalitarian societies—the gulag, the death camps—that we don't pay much attention to the fact that there is often an incremental process that led those societies to become places where such things could happen.

The view that fascism looks from the start like a nationwide prison camp rather than a fairly normal society can be comforting when facing an argument like mine. It's natural to wish that the two realities were so categorically different that, of course, "It couldn't happen here."

But as would-be dictators consolidate power, if they are training their sights on a democracy, things proceed fairly routinely in many areas in the earliest years. In the beginning, the horror, as W. H. Auden put it, is usually elsewhere, taking place while other people are going about their normal daily round. Peasants in Italy celebrated their harvest festivals in 1919 in Naples when Mussolini's *arditi* were beating bloody the local communists in Milan.[22] Journalist Joseph Roth, the star columnist for the *Frankfurter Zeitung*, filed glitzy reports on urban style and nightlife, on architecture and the avant-garde; he and his colleagues dwelt on the latest fashions and described the trendiest watering holes. As Roth rebutted rising anti-Semitism in print, Hitler was consolidating power around himself.[23] Victor Klemperer, a Jewish professor of French literature who kept a diary throughout the rise and fall of the Third Reich, cared for his garden, did repairs on his car, chatted with his Nazi neighbors, went to the movies with his wife, even as he became increasingly aware of persecution, arrests, theft of property, and new discriminatory laws; even as he was certain of an inevitable catastrophe.[24] That's what people do.

The neon lights were flashing outside nightclubs in Vienna right through the *Anschluss.* British travelogues for Italy and Germany from the 1930s depict jolly fascists sharing a nice Marsala with the writers in an Osteria. More recently, the day after the 2006 military coup in Thailand, tourists were posing for snapshots next to armed guards; sunbathers were still at the beach.[25] Most of the tourists didn't bother to go home even after martial law was declared. Such scenes show that contemporaries often experience a brighter picture of what is going on than what the history to be written in the future will reveal. It's as if societies continue to party upstairs while the foundations of the house crumble beneath them.

At first, Nazi Germany would not have looked, on the surface, so unrecognizable to us: Germans still, for a time, saw an independent judiciary; lawyers—even human rights lawyers; working journalists—even political satirists; criticism of Nazis in cabarets and theatre; and professors still teaching critical thinking. There were hundreds of newspapers of all political colors; there were feminist organizations, abortion rights activists, sex education institutes, even gay rights organizations. These kinds of civil society organizations would become "co-ordinated" with Nazi ideology, or simply disemboweled—but as the shift was first taking place things looked in many ways, superficially, like an open modern society.[26]

Even later in the game, violent dictatorships keep many of the trappings of a civil society. It is a point of pride to do so. What they do not have—and everyone who works in the press, the judiciary, the universities, the theatre, the electoral system, and so on, understands the rules about this—is freedom.

Americans don't get this at all, but other countries who have experienced dictatorships either near them or over them do get it: Journalists in Brazil and Argentina know exactly what the difference is between publishing a newspaper in freedom and publishing the same newspaper while looking over one's shoulder. The fact that we are unaware that a dictatorship can be incremental leaves us terribly vulnerable right now. Even educated American people think that if the press is publishing and Congress is legislating, all is well; but those things are often still happening right up to the point of no return in a closing democracy—and they keep happening, in neutered form, even after a violent dictatorship has been established.

A shift toward violent dictatorship does not need to look like people being fed into ovens; historically, it looked like that exactly once, and that was less than a decade after the Nazis gained power. A violent dictatorship almost never looks like that. At first, it can simply look like people weighing their words. At its turning point, it can simply look like a high-profile arrest for "treason" or a handful of arrests for "espionage"—even as tourists still flock to monuments and celebrities are still being photographed at clubs.

We are not in danger of a military coup. But home-grown American versions of the same steps that all dictators have advanced may yet create an America in which all our institutions are intact—but functioning weakly; in which citizens have in theory the right to dissent, and some may do so mutedly, but most are afraid to exercise that right robustly; in which the press is subdued, the opposition is pulling its punches, and people are worried about expressing their true opinions, because it may cost them their jobs, or worse. This would not be Munich in 1938, but it would be an America with another kind of culture than the one we have taken as our birthright: a culture in which the pendulum still exists, but the people's will cannot move it more than slightly.

We still have time to turn back the tide. What we do not have is leisure. A movement of citizens on the left and right have both begun to build what is essentially a democracy movement in America: the American Freedom Agenda and the American Freedom Campaign are trying to awaken the nation to these dangers and turn citizens into those leading the charge to defend the nation. The AFA created a legislative package to repeal or modify restrictive laws and restore liberty. We must roll back the laws that are associated with the opening of the door into darkness.

If we fail to act, we could face an America in which we still have Friday night football games and Fourth of July fireworks, Wal-Mart and The Food Network and the Statue of Liberty—but an America in which people who publish classified documents might go to jail and people who go to jail might not come out the same; an America with the same TV shows and video games, and even the same schedule of elections—but one in which you can lose your job if you say to a colleague that you voted against the grain; an America that looks much the same on the surface—but in which we no longer have real freedom.

It could easily become an America that is quieter and more frightened. And a quiet, frightened American citizenry does mean the end of the America the Founders created.

For a little while, we still have the power to stop that from happening.

—CHAPTER TWO —

INVOKE *an* EXTERNAL *and* INTERNAL THREAT

Fear is the foundation of most governments; but it is so sordid and brutal a passion, and renders men, in whose breasts it predominates, so stupid and miserable, that Americans will not be likely to approve of any political institution which is founded on it.

JOHN ADAMS

After September 11, 2001, we Americans learned in dramatic new ways that we were facing a terrifying external threat. We saw it in the carnage in lower Manhattan, but the administration also used a new set of phrases that defined for us a new reality. "Evildoers" who envied us and hated our freedoms were determined to annihilate us. By October 2001, the USA PATRIOT Act—that in the end, when it became law, topped 400 pages—rushed through Congress. Lawmakers passed it overwhelmingly—though many said that they had scarcely read it. Some remarked that it would have seemed unpatriotic to resist passing the law.[1]

White House rhetoric elaborated on the all-encompassing nature of the terrorist threat: it was an "axis of evil." ("Axis" is Mussolini's coinage; in 1936 he first offered the simile of an axis to describe the fascist states' collaboration).[2] By March 2003, with the invasion of Iraq, it was common for administration spokespeople to refer to Muslim terrorists as "evil." (Our allies, said the White House, were the countries of the "New Europe"—a phrase Hitler coined to describe Axis powers.)

By 2006 Bush was comparing Osama bin Laden to Lenin and Hitler; bin Laden posed "a threat to civilization" itself.[3] The White

House deployed the term *Islamofascism* to convey the idea that this global, ever-growing, and ever-shifting enemy wished to enslave us utterly.[4] Bush said that we were now committed to a global "war on terror." This war is eternal in time and space, with no endpoint at which you can say "We have won" or "We have lost." The "evildoers" want a "global caliphate," and the battlefield is the whole world. Bush speechwriter Michael Gerson wrote an essay in *Newsweek* that invoked the specter that terrorists representing "Islamic fascism" are seeking technologies to make "radical Islam a global power, allowing new killing on an unimagined scale."[5]

All those who seek to close down an open society invoke a terrifying external threat. Why is it so important for such leaders to whip up this kind of terror in a population?

Free citizens will not give up freedom for very many reasons, but it is human nature to be willing to trade freedom for security. People fear chaos and violence above all. Before 1922 in Italy and before 1933 in Germany, citizens of those nations suffered from mayhem playing out on the streets, and labored in economies ravaged by inflation and war.[6] In both Italy and Germany, many citizens were eventually relieved when fascists came to power because they believed that order would be restored.

But we are not wracked by rioting in the streets or a major depression here in America today. That is why the success that the Bush administration has had in invoking "Islamofascism" is so insidious: We have been willing to trade our key freedoms for a promised state of security in spite of our living in conditions of overwhelming stability, affluence, and social order. This is quite a feat in the annals of such victories: It is unprecedented to strip people of key freedoms in an atmosphere of bourgeois equilibrium. It takes potent mythologizing.

All fascist leaders tell citizens a story of an encircling global threat that is evil incarnate: "Fascists need a demonized enemy against which to mobilize followers," writes political theorist

Robert O. Paxton in *The Anatomy of Fascism.* Each culture, he writes, identifies its own national enemy.[7] Paxton points out that once an enemy has been identified, the elites create myths inflaming the fears that the population begins to suffer from in relation to this "other." The "enemy" is functional: What matters to a fascist leader is not to get *rid* of the enemy but rather to *maintain* an enemy.[8] (Because this is what really counts, Arendt points out that the "enemy" status can be shifted from group to group: when the Nazis had overcome the "enemy" represented by Jews, they moved on to demonize the Poles.)[9]

There is no reason the external enemy can't be real. International terrorism aimed at the West is all too real. Often fascist leaders invoke a threat that has elements of truth as its basis—but a truth that is distorted to their purposes. Fascist leaders, Paxton writes, do not elaborate a philosophy so much as a "mood" that whips up what he calls "the mobilizing passions" of the population: "At bottom is a passionate nationalism," he points out. "Allied to it is a conspiratorial and Manichean view of history as a battle between good and evil camps, between the pure and the corrupt, in which one's own community or nation has been the victim." These attitudes, he argues, form the "emotional lava that set fascism's foundations." Among the themes that fascist elites develop when they are driving toward an authoritarian system are:

- A sense of overwhelming crisis beyond the reach of any traditional solutions; . . .
- The belief that one's group is a victim, a sentiment that justifies any actions, without legal or moral limits, against its enemies, both internal and external; . . .
- The superiority of the leader's instincts over abstract and universal reason.[10]

Fascist leaders invariably describe this external threat as being global; impure; secretive; able to assume "harmless" camouflage that lets its members infiltrate ordinary society. They always portray this enemy as being backed by powerful international financiers who operate in subterranean ways, and as being capable of and intent upon destroying everything that the citizens of that society hold most dear. The threat is described as hydralike: If you cut off one of its heads, two more grow in its place.

Italian fascists used this tactic: In 1919 they warned that "Where there were external enemies, now there are internal foes. On one side real Italians, lovers of their country. On the other, their enemies, the cowards who seek to blow to pieces our national grandeur." By 1922, a fascist newspaper urged Italian women to get used to *Arditi* bloodshed, because death squads were necessary in order to rescue Italy from the "Bolshevik beast."[11] Italian fascist mythmaking exaggerated real dangers that Italy truly faced.

Weimar Germany, too, faced obvious dangers: not a Jewish conspiracy, of course, but multiple crises indeed. The Versailles treaty had humiliated veterans and eviscerated the industrial base of the nation; inflation was rampant, as was violent crime; many people felt that the moral base of their society was crumbling; their allegiances to Parliamentary processes were weak; and many Germans romanticized the "good old days" of the stable rule of Chancellor Otto von Bismarck. Violent street brawls erupted continually between Communists and Social Democrats on one side, and Brownshirts and Free Corps veterans on the other. Between 1924 and 1933, propagandists for the rising National Socialist party took these real threats and embellished them. Dangers were everywhere, they wrote; good Germans had been "stabbed in the back" by "November traitors" who had sold out their nation and enslaved its citizens to the humiliating Treaty of Versailles.[12] To real threats, these propagandists added fantasy ones: an urban, degenerate "Jewish influence" was undermining the values of pure-blooded Germans: they faced "the hydra of the black and red International, of Jews...."[13]

(Our own Presidents in the past have sometimes stirred up this fear of a shadowy internal and external threat: When faced the possibility of war with France in the 1790s, President John Adams suggested that the many French refugees in the country at that time posed a threat to social order and a danger of subversion, and implied that they were domestic traitors.)

The Rise of Hitler

Many of us have the impression that the Nazi seizure of power had a certain nightmare inevitability about it: We tend to see Nazism as an incomprehensible evil that subsumed Germany like a metaphysical whirlwind or a Biblical curse.

But that frame doesn't help us learn the lessons that we need.

Hitler could never have ascended to power as he did if the Reichstag had not first cravenly, but legally, weakened Germany's system of checks and balances. Lawmakers who were not Nazis—who in fact were horrified by Nazis—unwittingly opened the door for Nazis to overturn the rule of law, and did so before the Nazis even came formally to power.[14]

The Nazis rose to power in a living, if battered, democracy, through a day-by-day accretion of decisions—a set of tactics: "Contemporaries could not see things as clearly as we can, with the gift of hindsight: they could not know in 1930 what was to come in 1933, they could not know in 1933 what was to come in 1939 or 1942 or 1945," writes historian Richard J. Evans. But Evans also writes that "[D]evelopments that seem inevitable in retrospect were by no means so at the time, and in writing this book I have tried to remind the reader repeatedly that things could easily have turned out very differently to the way they did at a number of points. . . ."[15]

Hitler's predecessor, Reich Chancellor Heinrich Brüning, was not a National Socialist; he was a centrist. But he tampered with the framework of German democracy, reduced the power of the Parliament, and restricted civil liberties in a way that Nazis seized upon. Increasingly, the Republic was governed by emergency decree. The erosion of the rule of law unbolted the door for Hitler, and Hitler then used the law to burst it open and let the flood ensue.[16]

Hitler's Germany was no anarchic state: He used to law to legitimate virtually everything he did. Hitler often boasted that "We will overthrow Parliament in a legal way through legal means. Democracy will be overthrown with the tools of democracy."[17] "I can say clearly," he announced at a Nuremberg rally in 1934, "that the basis of the National Socialist state is the National Socialist law code." He called Nazi Germany "this state of order, freedom and law."[18]

Dictators can rise in a weakened democracy even with a minority of popular support. Hitler never won a majority: In the election in 1932, only 13.1 million Germans voted for the Nazi party. Although National Socialism was the largest single party, the Nazis had fewer seats in government than the combined opposition parties did. At that point they could still have been defeated.[19] Their numbers declined further in the next election.

At that critical time, Brownshirts waged a campaign of violence against Nazi Party opponents in the streets. A sense of crisis descended on the country. A coalition of conservatives united to provoke a constitutional crisis in Parliament as well. Lawmakers then engaged in frenzied negotiations to head off civil war. The conservative majority still believed at that point that if Hitler were appointed Reich Chancellor they would be able to control him. They made a deal: Hitler was sworn in as Reich Chancellor *entirely legally* on January 30, 1933.

But Nazis directed events to cascade rapidly after that: They staged torchlight marches while all marches by the Communist opposition were forbidden. When thousands of citizens marched against the new government nonetheless, police arrested their leaders. Twenty opposition newspapers took issue with the new Nazi leadership—but then the papers were banned; local authorities cracked down on free assembly across the country.[20]

Soon, Germans learned of a terrorist threat: The Reichstag was set on fire on February 27, 1933. That would be like someone trying to set fire to the Capitol. A disturbed young Dutch Communist, Marinus van der Lubbe, was accused of having set the fire. Some historians believe the Nazis engineered this attack themselves.

First, Nazi leader Hermann Goering informed Germany that it was now on a "war footing." Goering warned the nation that the Reichstag fire was just part of a larger plot: Communist terrorists, he said, had planned to poison the water supply and kidnap the families of government ministers. He claimed also to have evidence that these shadowy terrorists were planning bombing attacks on railroads, electrical works, and other infrastructure sites. These threats were never substantiated, but the nation was terrified nonetheless.[21]

The Nazi Reich Minister of the Interior, Wilhelm Frick, introduced "clause 2": It suspended parts of the German constitution. It shut down freedoms of expression and of the press and freedom of assembly. Clause 2 also gave police forces the power to hold people in custody indefinitely and without a court order. The law, and cowed lawmakers, had well prepared the way.[22]

At last, Hitler told the Cabinet that an amendment to the Constitution was required, the Enabling Act, which would allow him permanently to circumvent some powers of the Parliament. It was now legal for the state to tap citizens' phones and open their mail.[23]

Appalled at the terrorist threat, and not wanting to be seen as unpatriotic, there was little debate: lawmakers of all parties passed the Enabling Act by a wide majority: 441 to 94. The constitution remained, but from then on, Hitler could govern by decree.

Joseph Stalin too used the "internal and external threat" narrative. Party functionary Sergei Kirov was assassinated in Moscow in 1934, probably with Stalin's blessing. Stalin blamed the murder on counterrevolutionary "terrorists." He warned Russians of a worldwide conspiracy of capitalist-imperialist villains determined to wage a war against the country, and working in concert with an internal network of other "counterrevolutionary terrorists," "assassins," and "wreckers."[24] The fear engendered by that story set the stage for the mass arrests of 1937 to 1938.

The hydra narrative became boilerplate for would-be dictators: During the Cold War, Communist leaders urged East German and Czech citizens to beware a bloodthirsty cabal of "capitalist imperialists" as well as domestic "enemies of the revolution."[25]

In September 1973, General Pinochet's military junta displayed a cache of arms on television and told Chilean citizens that the Unidad Popular (whom they called "terrorists") planned to assassinate many of Chile's military leaders in one blow.[26]

Is the "Islamofascism" threat new, or is the way we are hearing about it new—for us? The Clinton administration was profoundly worried about Islamic terrorism: The bombing of the USS *Cole* and the first attack on the World Trade Center took place on Clinton's watch. But the language that President Clinton and his State Department used to describe the same terrorists then was quite different from the language we hear today, and 9/11 itself does not explain the difference: Clinton's team used language about a serious geopolitical threat, but we did not hear mythologizing about a hydra of "evil" and "evildoers."

Extremist Islamic terrorists do seek to harm us. But Bush has universalized the fanatical claims of the most fanatical elements of the threat. The United Kingdom and Spain have suffered grave terrorist assaults, but those nations have, in contrast, described the same people and the same threat in more prosaic language. British and Spanish citizens think they are facing a serious security concern; Americans, however, fear that the same threat can bring about the end of civilization.

The "Security-Industrial Complex"

America is not driven by pure ideologies the way that fascist Italy and Nazi Germany were. In America, profit drives events where ideology does not: Within days of the 9/11 attacks, security companies were lobbying airport and government officials to invest in new technologies of surveillance. Six years later, the surveillance industry is huge business: "[S]urveillance technologies are emerging as one of the ripest plums for companies to pluck in the new 'anti-terrorism biz.'"[27] In 2003, business writers estimated that this burgeoning industry was worth $115 billion a year. If trends continued, they estimated, the windfall from new surveillance and security demands would bring in $130 to $180 billion a year by 2010.

Lockheed Martin, Acxiom, ChoicePoint, and other companies have sharply increased their investment in lobbying for a piece of this profit: ChoicePoint alone quadrupled the money it put into lobbying after 9/11. A 2003 study found that 569 companies had registered Homeland Security lobbyists after 9/11.[28] *The New York Times* reported that "the major defense contractors want to move into the homeland security arena in a big way."[29] Dr. William Haseltine, who sits on the boards of many of the organizations that analyze this industry, including the Trilateral Commission and The Brookings Institution, and who is one of the founders of the American Freedom Campaign, says that the "security-industrial complex" rivals the "military-industrial complex" in influencing policy.[30]

Peace is bad for business. When the former Soviet Union fell apart, the U.S. defense industry was staring into the face of a falling market share: To grow, it would have to find a new enemy. It would also help if it expanded its product line from building fighter jets to the newfangled demand for applications involving surveillance.

Dr. Haseltine points out that the Department of Homeland Security has, like the Defense Department, an external corollary in private industry; so the relationships between the two departments are now institutionalized.[31] The Department of Homeland Security will be almost impossible to dismantle whether or not it is successful in protecting Americans: An $115-billion-a-year industry can exert major pressure on policy-making, and the Department of Homeland Security is not going to go away, even if tomorrow all the Muslim terrorists in the world were to lay down their arms.

But what if Islamic terrorism does subside? A foreign enemy's actions will always be unpredictable. But you can also identify a more reliable domestic enemy in need of surveillance: us. A powerful lobby is now served by policies in which government increasingly designates U.S. *citizens* as potential security threats, which in turn creates a demand for more and more costly high-tech watching.

The ACLU is measured in describing how this profit potential affects legislation: "It is not possible to determine the overall extent to which private-sector lobbying has actually driven the government's push for increased surveillance, as opposed to simply helping companies fight for a pieces of a pre-determined government pie. . .but in at least some cases, major new impetus for surveillance-friendly policies has clearly come from the private sector. . . . There is much more money to be made providing complex, cutting-edge technological solutions to security problems," they note, than there is in solutions that may be more truly effective but cheaper, such as strengthening cockpit doors. "It would be a double tragedy," their report continues, "if the emerging surveillance-industrial complex were not only to lobby for increased surveillance of Americans, but also to divert resources from security measures that would be far more likely to be effective in protecting Americans from attacks."[32]

So: the state has now identified, mythologized, and institutionalized an external and internal threat—indefinitely. Who is caught in the middle between the mythologies of the external and internal enemies? Ordinary Americans—us.

— CHAPTER THREE —

ESTABLISH SECRET PRISONS

No person shall be . . . deprived of life, liberty, or property, without due process of law . . .

THE FIFTH AMENDMENT TO THE CONSTITUTION

In all criminal prosecutions, the accused shall enjoy the right to a speedy and public trial, by an impartial jury . . . and to be informed of the nature and cause of the accusation; to be confronted with the witnesses against him; to have compulsory process for obtaining witnesses in his favor, and to have the Assistance of Counsel for his defense.

THE SIXTH AMENDMENT

The Magna Carta was signed in 1215. Since then, our Western legal tradition has held that everyone deserves some kind of judicial process before being thrown into prison. This simple yet radical notion that you cannot be unaccountably imprisoned is the cornerstone of all democracy. We Americans expect that we can't be thrown into jail without hope of getting out. That faith is so essential a part of our liberty that we scarcely think about it.

This guarantee that you can't be randomly jailed is strengthened by the concept of habeas corpus. This is the law, dating from 1679, that undergirds our freedom as Americans. The phrase comes from the Latin; it is a writ "to have the body." Having the right to habeas corpus means that if they grab you and throw you in jail, you have the right to see the evidence against you, face your accusers, and have a hearing before an impartial judge or jury to establish whether you actually committed the crime of which you are accused. In short, it means that if you are innocent, there is hope that you can prove that you are, and hope that you can eventually get out. It means your innocence protects you.

Your innocence does not protect you in a dictatorship.

Just as habeas corpus, or some equivalent procedure, is the cornerstone of virtually every democracy, so a secret prison system without habeas corpus is the cornerstone of every dictatorship. You cannot push an open society into submission without a secret prison or, more effective still, a system of secret prisons. By "secret prison," I mean a prison system that is not accountable and that is beyond the rule of law. Building a secret prison system beyond the rule of law permits everything else that follows. Without the real threat of such a secret prison system, citizens speak up, activists are forceful, and democracy is stubborn.

The classic secret prison system starts out modestly and metastasizes. Initially the government targets people seen by the rest of the population as being "evil": dangerous radicals or outright criminals. At this stage, the prisons—even the mistreatment and torture of prisoners—are publicized, to general acceptance or even approval: Cartoons in the German press from 1931 to 1933 made light of prisoner abuse.[1] Early on, the secret prisons and even this abuse make citizens feel safer: They can't imagine that they themselves might ever be subjected to mistreatment.

And then there is a "mission creep"—always. The thick black line that has separated "us" from "them" starts to blur. The secret prison system expands, slowly or quickly but inexorably, to seize civil-society leaders, journalists, clergy, and the political opposition. I challenge you to name a time and place when this did not happen.

Early on, this mission creep is seldom evident. There is a strong, if unconscious, psychological denial among citizens at this stage. Because there is now a two-caste system, and because most people are in the protected caste, a kind of magical thinking makes many people feel more secure as they witness "others" being sent into brutal detention. This is the regressive seduction of fascism—a "Daddy wouldn't harm me" kind of thinking, a sense of privilege as Daddy's state-sanctioned ire and even violence are directed at others outside the circle of safety. Then, if they are working in a democracy, leaders seeking a fascist shift acclimate citizens to an ever-lowered bar for the acceptance of state torture. (The Fox TV show *24* depicts torture as entertainment. The producers recently noted that torture is no longer shocking, let alone news.[2])

Secret Prisons Metastasize

Why should Americans worry about Guantánamo? Because history shows us that building a secret prison opens a Pandora's box in Hell. In the mission creep I mentioned, citizens start to see well-publicized reports of arrests of people whose status begins to blurs the thick black line that had been established between "us" and "them."[3] This is a sensitive time: if the authorities move too fast, and arrest people with whom ordinary citizens identify too early, there will be a backlash. But if the leaders seeking a fascist shift get away with these arrests, a citizen backlash stalls. Believe it or not, that is where we are right now in America.

In the endgame of a fascist shift, deportations to the secret prison claim citizens at the heart of civil life. It is always the same cast, in regime after regime: opposition leaders, outspoken clergy, union leaders, well-known performers, publishers, and journalists.

At this stage, the regime starts to call critics "enemies of the state," "enemies of the people," "traitors," "criminals," and "spies." At this point there are likely to be show trials where evidence is withheld from the prisoner, or secret trials, for "security purposes." Citizens are gradually stripped of elements of due process. The independent judicial system is bypassed altogether because a "people's court" or military tribunal system has been revived or newly established alongside it. The message at this point is that no one is safe, and by then it is pretty much over. This stage of the shift tends to happen very fast.

(The same lesson—you don't need Nazi-style death camps to subdue a nation, only a network of indefinite detention and torture camps set up as a backdrop—has been learned well by many dictators. Alfredo Stroessner of Paraguay—who offered his nation as a haven for Nazis[4]—used this part of the ten steps, as did dictators in Argentina, Brazil, Indonesia, Nicaragua, Uruguay, and Guatemala.[5] Many of these dictators established sadistic prison camps; used paramilitary death squads; "disappeared" critics; stripped prisoners of the right to trial; targeted opposition leaders, academics, journalists, scientists, performers, and clergy; orchestrated mass arrests; and practiced torture directed by the state. Even in "merely" authoritarian regimes such as Morocco and Egypt, which don't have torture camps along the same lines, it's well known among citizens that prisoners die "accidentally" in brutal interrogations. These deaths also intimidate civil society.[6])

We should worry about the men held at Guantánamo because history shows that stripping prisoners of their rights is intoxicating not only to leaders but to functionaries at every level of society. Professor Philip Zimbardo, in *The Lucifer Effect*, shows once again how easy it is for even decent people to become desensitized and act as instruments of evil. Once a government crosses that line, it's easier for would-be dictators to portray such demands as the right to a lawyer, the chance to see the evidence against you, and the right to be heard by an impartial judge as trivial impediments to a "national security" goal as they choose to define it, rather than as essential rights for all.

The historical record shows without doubt that after that has happened, secret prisons start to operate with ever-more severe penalties, ever-greater violence, and always less accountability. So many regimes have fostered this development that it seems to prove a dark potential inherent in human nature. Even well-informed people aren't always sure why habeas corpus and due process in general are not expendable in a time of crisis. We forget that these processes are intimately related to our own physical safety in America. "Due process" and "the rule of law" are not, it turns out, dry formalities; if they remain robust, when leaders are seeking a dictatorship, they can save our lives.

In Mussolini's Italy, the prison system was never as brutal as that of Germany and Russia, but Mussolini sent tens of thousands of political prisoners into internal exile (*confino*) nonetheless; thousands died in the prisons.[7]

One of the first things the Nazis did was to establish prisons in legal "outer space," often in basements, guarded by SS officers who were not accountable to the state; they rounded up communists, criminals and anarchists, and tortured them. By 1933, when Hitler was Chancellor, ordinary Germans were taken to these torture sites as well. On March 20 of that year, SS leader Heinrich Himmler announced that a concentration camp for political prisoners would be opened—Dachau, just outside of Munich. Within thirty days, the SA and SS had rounded up, arrested, imprisoned, tortured, or often simply shot dead tens of thousands of Communists, Social Democrats, other opposition leaders, labor leaders, journalists, and clergy. That whole year, storm troopers continued to make these arrests.[8]

The first concentration camps, such as Oranienberg, received the political prisoners. In 1933, most of the 27,000 detainees were there because they were political opponents of the regime.[9]

So Hitler came to power in a democracy that at first still possessed an independent judiciary, human rights lawyers, an accountable military, and a legitimate prison system. But, in a matter of months, he had deployed a paramilitary force answerable to him; set in motion an alternative system of tribunals in which his representatives served as judge, jury, and executioner; and established a network of illegitimate prisons where torture took place. Those steps were enough to create the conditions from which there was no turning back. To make sure that the remaining vestiges of democratic process would not deter him from attaining absolute power, Hitler passed a law "appoint[ing] himself as Supreme Judge with the power to imprison or execute individuals without benefit of trial."[10]

The mass arrests of 1933 were so effective in quelling the population that within several years, the prisons held less than a quarter of the prisoners they had before. Many had been killed, but another reason for the drop in population is that, by then, opposition had simply withered. The entire society—those who agreed with Nazis and those who did not—was "co-ordinated" under the banner of Nazi ideology, and any dissent now carried a mortal risk.[11]

The Nazis did not need formal extermination camps to control the population. The formal extermination camps that murdered millions, with which most of us are more familiar, were not established until the very eve of the war. The prisons of the mid-1930s, in contrast, terrorized people "only" through widely publicized violent interrogation, beatings, deliberate denial of medical care, and informal murder committed by guards who knew there was no chance of their being punished. That was enough to silence dissent.[12]

Stalin's Terror also shows that secret prisons and torture metastasize. The prison camps of the gulag became ever more numerous, more violent, and more lawless: "The first codes of Soviet law categorically forbade the use of penal methods that could be considered torture. . . . In 1937 all these liberal systems were abolished. . . . The corrective-labor camps were turned into hard-labor camps, calculated not so much to correct as to destroy the prisoners. . . . Camps for special punishment . . . became virtual death camps."[13]

It took only six years for Stalin, the NKVD police, the ever-more brutal network of prisons, and arrests of tens of thousands of citizens—the usual suspects—to terrorize the country. With the prison system intact, once charges of "sabotage" or "attempted rebellion" began to fly, any Soviet citizen could find him or herself accused on the basis of a stray remark of being a "traitor," a "state and political criminal," or a "conciliator." Then he or she could be held without seeing evidence, tried in a show trial, imprisoned, tortured, or even executed.

Guantánamo

> *Excessive bail shall not be required . . . nor cruel and unusual punishments inflicted.*
>
> The Eighth Amendment

It is well documented that the Bush administration set the stage for torture to take place at Abu Ghraib prison in Iraq, after Major General Geoffrey Miller was sent to "Gitmo-ize" interrogations. Michael Ratner and Ellen Ray's report, *Guantánamo: What the World Should Know*, documents the fact that the White House institutionalized torture at Guantánamo too, long before the administration asked Congress to make the abuse legal in 2006. "Guantánamo is a twenty-first century Pentagon experiment that was, in fact, outlawed by the Geneva Conventions of 1949," says Ratner, who has faced death threats because he helps to represent the detainees.

Nazi Germany is hardly irrelevant to the Guantánamo debate: the Geneva Conventions were revised in 1949 because of world revulsion against Nazi practices. "[Guantánamo] is similar in purpose to the German World War II operations that led to the [Geneva Conventions] ban: it is an interrogation camp, and interrogation camps are completely and flatly illegal."[14]

In spite of the Supreme Court's 2006 ruling, *Hamdan v. Rumsfeld*, that the protections of the Geneva Conventions apply to inmates at Guantanamo, violent abuse, ranging from waterboarding to beatings to sexual humiliation, has been commonplace there. According to *Newsweek*, Guantánamo developed a "72-point matrix for 'stress and duress. . . .' These included the use of harsh heat or cold; withholding food; hooding for days at a time; naked isolation in cold, dark cells for more than 30 days, and threatening (but not biting) by dogs. It also permitted limited use of 'stress positions' designed to subject detainees to rising levels of pain."[15]

Torture creates the division between speech and silence when people are assessing what they will personally risk. Legal torture, as I mentioned, changes everything. The existence of a secret prison where torture takes place moves the state's threat closer to the body of every citizen and sets the bar of courage higher for everyone when it comes to speaking out.

People concerned about civil liberties try to alert others by reminding them of the last repressive era in the United States, the McCarthy witch hunts. We need to get past that frame to understand where we are now. The McCarthy threat is a cakewalk compared to the threats against dissent that are legally possible now. Citizens who challenged the McCarthy blacklisters, men and women such as Arthur Miller and Lillian Hellman, were courageous; but—not to diminish their courage—no one speaking out at that time risked being driven mad by years of isolation in a narrow cell. They risked nothing more physically brutal than the end of a career.

Playwright, democracy activist, and former Czech President Václav Havel knows about how violence resets the bar of courage: He was held as a political prisoner for four and a half years in a prison that was uncomfortable, but that did not use torture. When asked about his courage, he notes rightly, "None of us know in advance how we will behave. . . . I don't know, for example, what I would do if I were physically tortured."[16]

Havel's courage helped to free Czechoslovakia; if he had been tortured, would he and his fellow Czechs still be living in a closed society?

Who are these "evildoers" being tortured today by the United States?

According to a Seton Hall University study, most of the

Guantánamo prisoners are innocent, and were swept up by Northern Alliance warlords in Afghanistan simply because the United States had offered bounties of up to $5000 per prisoner, a major sum for that area. The warlords often simply gave the United States names of neighbors with whom they had disputes, or even of random villagers, to get the money.[17] (These are the same warlords, by the way, who raped and brutalized their own people before the advent of the equally brutal Taliban.)

The prisoners were then, according to Ratner and Ray, "kept in metal shipping containers, so tightly packed that they had to ball themselves up, and the heat was unbearable. . . . The people inside were suffocating, so the Northern Alliance soldiers shot holes into the containers, killing some of the prisoners inside."[18] Some of the men who survived were taken, blindfolded and shackled, onto transport planes, where they were chained belly-down on the floor for twenty-four hours. Forbidden to go to the bathroom, the prisoners lay in their own urine and feces until they arrived at Guantánamo and were put in cells.[19] (Stalin's prisoners, transported by train to the gulags, were also forced to lie publicly in their own urine and feces—a part of the journey that was as horrifying to them as the more overt forms of violence.)

In the camp, squads of U.S. military personnel "beat people up, sometimes quite severely." Red Cross reports, which are not public, have leaked: prisoners were stripped, short-shackled to a chain on the floor, and forced to kneel or stand for hours during interrogations. They were kept in extremes of heat and cold—sometimes at temperatures of 110 degrees. At Camp X-Ray, the prisoners were kept in the "dog-run-like cages," exposed to the elements and to beatings by the IRF (Immediate Reaction Forces). Meals and medical care could be withheld from prisoners who refused to cooperate.

The psychological torture is, the prisoners report, the most painful of all: They are told that there is no way out unless they confess. "[T]hey [U.S. forces] also intimidated prisoners with family photos. . .threatening that things would happen to the prisoner's family unless the prisoner talked."

Guantánamo is growing: the dog-run-like cells of 2002 have been built up into formal cells. Two new camps, Romeo and Tango, have been built to be total isolation camps.[20] Prolonged isolation triggers psychosis even in mentally healthy prisoners: Every camp in the Soviet Gulag had an isolation block for prisoners who didn't cooperate, as in Guantánamo.[21]

Yet, as one otherwise compassionate friend of mine put it, "That's not my issue." Most Americans have found it difficult to worry much about the "tough" or "harsh" interrogations of people who, they think, are probably terrorists.

The Founders would have been shocked at these attitudes. They did care about the just treatment of prisoners, even of the most despised political prisoners: "There is one example of this violation in Virginia, of a most striking and shocking nature," said Virginia Attorney General Edmund Randolph, to the Constitutional Convention. "[A]n example so horrid that, if I conceived my country would passively permit a repetition of it, dear as it is to me, I would seek means of expatriating myself from it. A man [Josiah Phillips, a political prisoner], who was then a citizen, was deprived of his life thus: from a mere reliance on general reports, [he was accused of] several crimes. . . . He was attained very speedily and precipitately, without any proof better than vague reports. Without being confronted with his accusers and witnesses, without the privilege of calling for evidence in his behalf, he was sentenced to death, and was afterwards actually executed. . . . I cannot contemplate it without horror."[22]

"ACLU focus groups do not care about Guantánamo," says spokeswoman Emily Whitfield. "But when you tell them . . . that citizens can be seized on the street and kidnapped and shipped away to be tortured—it makes even Republican guys crazy."[23] What Whitfield is telling these Americans is true.

Even after Congress passed the Military Commissions Act of

2006, most Americans continue to assume that the only way one can be subjected to "harsh interrogations" or other abuse is if one is actively engaged in terrorist crimes against the United States. Even now, many well-informed people believe that you can't possibly be mistreated if you are a U.S. citizen.

But President Bush has claimed the "unilateral authority" to "arrest virtually anyone, anywhere, citizen or noncitizen, even in the United States, if he deemed them an enemy combatant," warns Ratner.[24] Any U.S. citizen can now be mistreated in various ways.

Two U.S. citizens, Yaser Hamdi and José Padilla, had already been taken as "enemy combatants," even before the Military Commissions Act was passed.

Hamdi, a 31-year-old born in Louisiana, wasn't physically tortured, but he was imprisoned in a navy brig without a trial *for three years*. He was unable to tell his family where he was; forbidden to speak to a lawyer; and could not see the evidence against him or receive a visit from the Red Cross. The Bush administration argued that they had to make this U.S. citizen believe he was utterly in the power of his interrogators, that his situation was hopeless and that he would never get out, in order to question him usefully.[25] When the Supreme Court insisted that this American citizen had to receive some kind of hearing, the administration simply let him go.[26] It is hard not to wonder if a hearing might have revealed that the evidence against him would not hold up.

José Padilla, a 36-year-old American citizen, was called an "enemy combatant." You probably heard of him as the "dirty bomber" because that's how his arrest saturated the airwaves: The administration asserted when they took him in that he had al-Qaeda connections, he planned to set off a dirty bomb, and he was also planning a series of natural gas explosions in apartment buildings.[27] Very scary.

(You probably didn't hear that none of those accusations appear in the indictment against him. In fact, *no* violent plot against the United States appears in the indictment.[28])

His lawyers say Padilla's interrogations included "hooding, stress positions, assaults, threats of imminent execution and the administration of 'truth serums'" (Guantánamo detainees also report receiving injections of some kind during interrogations).[29] José Padilla was entirely alone for these three years in a ten-cell wing of a South Carolina brig: He rarely had human contact except with his interrogator; his meals were slid to him through a slot; he was continually electronically monitored; his windows were blacked out; he had no clock or calendar; his mattress was taken away from him so that he had to sleep on a steel slab; and he became so passive that the brig's staff told his lawyer that Padilla was like "a piece of furniture."[30]

It took *twenty-one months* for the U.S. government to let him see his attorney. Dr. Angela Hegarty, of Creedmore Psychiatric Center, examined him before his trial; she said in an affidavit that he was not in a condition to help himself in his own defense because of his mental condition. Another psychiatrist who examined Padilla believes he may have suffered a brain injury as a result of his treatment.

In spite of his having become "like a piece of furniture," when Padilla finally emerged to see a dentist, he was chained; he had blackout goggles over his eyes and noise-blocking headphones covering his ears; and he was surrounded dramatically by guards wearing riot gear. By the way, his plea to the government's charges is "not guilty."[31] As of this writing, the president claims that he has the right to do this to you or me tomorrow—on the president's say-so alone.

Most people take it for granted that Bush's effort to establish a practice of torture or abuse is aimed at "real" terrorists.

But let's look more closely.

Throughout years of legal maneuvers, starting long before the September of 2006 victory in Congress, the Bush White House aggressively tried to redefine the level of abuse legally considered to be torture, and to keep the definition of "enemy combatant" broad and loose.

Throughout the litigation of these two cases involving U.S. citizens, Bush administration lawyers resisted *defining* "enemy combatant" with specificity.

This effort goes back to just six months after 9/11, to the Taft-Haynes Memo of March 22, 2002.[32] Bush requested this memo from his lawyers to support his claim that the Geneva Conventions should not apply to the conflict with al-Qaeda or the Taliban. The arguments are broad, the terms subjective, and the method is that of looking for loopholes to exempt people from protected status: Taft invokes arguments that "the [Civilians'] Convention could not of course cover *criminals or saboteurs*." Still another argument notes that the rights and privileges of the Convention can't apply to "unprivileged combatants engaged in '*unlawful belligerency*.'"[33]

In the wording of the 2002 "torture memo,"—Bybee-Gonzales August 1, 2002 memo re: Standards of conduct for interrogation—torture is laboriously underdefined.[34]

(When you are looking at suggestions of a fascist shift in a democracy, intention is important; drafts and memos reveal what the regime seeks, if it could be unconstrained.)

The "torture memo" also shows how far back this White House has sought to legalize abuse and how hard it has worked to do so. The memo is forty pages of densely worded legal argument in favor of allowing all kinds of horrific treatment of human beings. It concludes that:

> [Torture] covers only extreme acts. Severe pain is generally of the kind difficult for the victim to endure. Where the pain is physical, it must be of an intensity akin to that which accompanies serious physical injury such as *death or organ failure*. Severe mental pain requires suffering not just at the moment of infliction but it also requires lasting psychological harm, such as seen in mental disorders like post-traumatic stress disorder. Additionally, such severe mental pain can

> arise only from the predicate acts listed. . . . Because the acts inflicting torture are extreme, there is significant range of acts that though they might constitute cruel, inhuman, or degrading treatment or punishment fail to rise to the level of torture.[35] [*Italics mine*]

Why go to this level of grim acrobatics to legalize such savage activity?

Americans do not live in a bubble of immunity that most of us are sure protects us from the broad range of this administration's assertions. After Hamdi, legal scholar Lloyd C. Anderson noted, "[T]he rationale of the Hamdi decision—that the AUMF provides authority to detain—strongly suggests that the president has the authority to detain a United States citizen in the United States as an enemy combatant."[36]

The government's position is that even U.S. citizens can be held indefinitely without charge, and the president has reserved what he views as his right to mistreat those he detains. "Whatever is permitted under the president's broad assertion of power can be done to you," said my law professor friend. He explained that, until the Supreme Court rules otherwise, if it does—and please recall that several key decisions on civil liberties could have gone the other way by but a single vote—President Bush alone will continue to decide whom to detain and whether to charge them, no matter who they are. The president argues, most importantly, that the courts must uphold the detention of citizens even when there is no direct evidence against them. Mere declarations by government officials, the administration says, should suffice.

I asked my friend to explain this further. "The president in essence says he has the power to decide who should be detained as an 'enemy combatant,' and to hold them, without charge or trial, indefinitely," he said.

"Does this mean they can arrest a reporter? Or a critic?"

"They won't come for them this year," the professor remarked.

"But their arguments would permit them to take anyone, based essentially on their own say-so."[37]

Belligerents, *saboteurs*, *criminals*; these are Stalin's words.[38] More importantly, they are broad, loose categories. Vague, loose definitions of what a criminal is are typical of fascist legislation: The Nuremberg Laws of 1938, for instance, turned an ordinary German into a criminal if his girlfriend was Jewish, and turned a German Jew into a criminal if he or she displayed the German flag.[39] These laws don't proliferate simply to stamp out forbidden actions; rather, they act as a way to create a category of people and activities that are suddenly or unexpectedly criminalized as a way to ensnare and intimidate citizens.

Penalties in Germany escalated so that anyone who helped a Jew or who spoke up against the abuse of Jews and others targeted by the state eventually faced official opprobrium or, later, charges. This kind of proliferating taboo with criminal penalties is at work now against those Americans who speak up for the detainees. Lawyers representing detainees, as we will see, have had career setbacks, have been faced with threats of boycotts, and even been threatened with criminal charges.

We too, as U.S. citizens, face an increasingly elaborate tripwire. People who have "materially and purposely supported hostilities"—who could this be? Could it be a peace activist who asks Congress to cut funding for the Iraq war? Journalists reporting on classified information? A whistle-blowing civil servant?

"The Pentagon has made up a new term," says Ratner, "'enemy combatant'. . . This is a totalitarian system in which there are no checks or balances on the executive. The president can do whatever he wants, acting as a dictator. In this system the courts have no independent function and can't protect anybody's rights. . . . [With Military Order No. 1, Bush] issued a military order giving himself the power to run the country as a general."

But aren't U.S. citizens safe, protected by habeas corpus and the Constitution? "The Bush administration claimed," argues Ratner,

> . . . Under these claimed commander-in-chief powers [that] the president can . . . designate people enemy combatants and detain them for whatever reason he wants . . . there are no charges and prisoners have no lawyers, no family visits, no court reviews, no rights to anything, and no right to release until the mythical end to the "war on terror."[40]

"Fingerprints" from Other Prison Systems

Accounts of Stalin's gulag show parallels between the methods that Stalin used on political prisoners and the practices introduced by military interrogators in Guantánamo. The Communist Revolutionaries of 1917 were opposed to torture, having suffered it themselves at the hands of czarist forces. So in order for Stalin to promote the use of torture, he had to create new laws and form new attitudes. Eventually, "physical torture" in Stalin's secret prisons "was used with the complete approval of the central offices. Of course the policy did not spring up in a single day but developed gradually over several years," writes historian Roy Medvedev. Adhering even minimally to legal methods of investigation would not let Stalin do what he needed to do. So Stalin advocated that the NKVD use what he called "physical methods of influence" on prisoners.[41]

The Abu Ghraib photos emerged in April 2004. Americans were appalled. But in less than three years Americans went from being horrified by these photos to being accustomed enough to detainee abuse to let Congress pass the 2006 law. In less than three years, the White House went from rhetorically disavowing the use of torture to being confident enough openly to advance legislation to permit many cruel practices.

In 1937 the Soviet February–March Plenum changed the law to expand the use of torture. After that, the "most refined tortures" could be directed legally at "stubborn enemies of the people"[42]—which meant, remember, just about anyone. Whether one agreed or disagreed with Stalin's party line, one could also be charged with being an "enemy of the people."

Eugenia Ginzburg was a devoted communist, a teacher, and a mother of three. To her dismay, the NKVD accused her of being part of an "underground terrorist organization." She was sent to prison. She learned there from "Greta," another prisoner, that detainees were tortured into confessing:

> "They have special apparatus to produce . . . confession," [Greta tells Ginzburg].
>
> "Torture!" I exclaimed.
>
> Greta nodded sadly. "Night come, you hear."[43]

Stalin's torturers routinely led their prisoners to believe they would be killed in order to elicit their false confessions. (This tactic was used on Hamdi as well as on others by the United States.) The NKVD used dogs on prisoners. (So do we.)

Humiliation

Interrogators at Guantánamo humiliate prisoners: Prisoners' heads and beards are forcibly shaved as punishment[44]—an act as affronting to Muslims' sensibilities as was the forced shaving of the beards and peyos of Jews in Germany in the 1930s. Detainees also report that guards have spit in their food.[45]

Stalin's prisons used psychological humiliation: An NKVD interrogator would urinate in a glass and force the prisoner to drink it.[46] Prison memoirs recount other kinds of sexualized humiliations. (To the horror of women's rights activists, the Military Commissions Act of 2006 defines "rape narrowly—leaving it legal for an interrogator to force a female or male prisoner to strip, as well as legalizing many other methods to coerce, violate and degrade people sexually."[47] According to *Newsweek*, the Red Cross cites "acts of humiliation such as [detainees] being made to stand naked . . . with women's underwear over the head, while being laughed at by guards, including female guards." Notably, the Bush administration gave a private screening for Congress to show 1800 slides and videos of atrocities that the public would not see, including sexual ones.[48] So while by now everyone is scared of what can happen to people in U.S. military custody, Congress has seen what is scariest.)

At Guantánamo male prisoners have indeed been stripped naked, and both male and female guards looked in at them continually. Human rights organizations have multiple independent reports of male prisoners having been handled sexually by female guards.[49]

Standing Positions

We've all heard by now about the use at Guantánamo of the "stress position"—rephrased by the White House as the more benign-sounding "long-standing position." (Rumsfeld dismissively noted, when reports of the practice caused dismay, that he stands for eight to ten hours a day.)[50] In Guantánamo and other U.S.-held prisons, the prisoner in a "stress position" must remain standing for hours or days, as in the famous photo of the hooded Abu Ghraib prisoner standing, arms outstretched, on a steel box.

Stress positions or *long-standing positions* are euphemisms for a technique developed in Stalin's prisons and known as the dreaded "conveyor." In the gulag, agents forced prisoners to remain in one position for hours, without being allowed to sleep. P. A. Shabalkin's prison diary describes this: "The so-called conveyor is set up: the interrogators change but the prisoner stands or sits. For days. They kept me, for example, on the conveyor for eight days. They don't let you sleep. . . . But if you withstand the conveyor and don't crack, physical torture follows."[51]

Eugenia Ginzburg saw a prisoner being forced to stand for two days; when he still refused to sign a false confession, the NKVD took him to a "standing cell": "[I]t was a place so narrow that the prisoner could only stand upright with his hands at his sides. . . . We were so appalled that for two days we scarcely uttered a word."[52]

Does this forced standing yield good intelligence? Many memoirs of Stalin's Gulag confirm that after just days of experiencing the conveyor, innocent Soviet prisoners would sign anything.

Sleep Deprivation

President Bush defended the practice of depriving detainees of sleep. It sounds almost harmless. You wake them up? Big deal. It's not a spa.

Another survivor of Stalin's secret prisons, M. M. Ishov, wrote that Stalin's prisoners were also forbidden to sleep: "Everything was done to wear out the prisoners completely."[53] Again, after just a week of sleep deprivation, Stalin's prisoners would name any names—and make up names. The East German secret police used the same method, with similar results.

According to the classic psychiatric study, *Recovering Sanity: A Compassionate Approach to Understanding and Treating Psychosis*, by Edward M. Podvoll, prolonged sleep deprivation and isolation drive sane people mad.

Use of Water

Interrogators at Guantánamo use "waterboarding," a torture invented in the Spanish Inquisition.[54] The gulag used water against prisoners as well: Guards at Iaroslav Prison threw a female prisoner into an isolation cell and drenched her with ice water with a hose. The NKVD poured icy water on uncooperative prisoners held on shipboard prisons.[55]

Extremes of Heat and Cold

Prisoners at Guantánamo report suffering from extremes of temperature.[56] Manipulating temperature extremes was common in the gulag too: Ishov reported that the cells were deliberately kept at about 44 degrees. Stalin's prisoners were held in the basement near central heating pipes.[57]

Danger to Those Who Help

In a fascist shift, security forces predictably begin to detain and try those who are "other," and gradually open the noose to include those more and more like "us;" David Hicks, a white, English-speaking Australian, was the third detainee to be tried by the U.S. military tribunals. You can also predict from the Fascist playbook that lawyers for detainees will get into trouble.

The Military Tribunals have begun, and they are increasingly dangerous to the military JAG lawyers for the detainees and others speaking up on their behalf. Penalties for such advocates began with career setbacks and are escalating into criminal charges or worse. In April 2007 the Justice Department asked a federal appeals court to "remove some of the last shreds of legal representation" available to the prisoners. It wants to let military and intelligence officers read the lawyers' mail to the prisoners; limit their visits to only three; and "allow government officials—on their own authority—to deny lawyers access to the evidence used to decide whether an inmate is an 'illegal enemy combatant.'" The administration also accused the lawyers of improperly relaying messages to the news media—a charge frighteningly close to one that had another attorney, Lynne Stewart, facing 30 years in prison.[58]

These lawyers are carrying on a noble tradition: At the height of anti-Tory hysteria, Alexander Hamilton chose to serve as attorney to represent one of the most hated categories of people of the time, a supporter of the Crown. Hamilton did so in the face of an angry mob, knowing that he risked the end of his career, because he believed so strongly in rule of law. John Adams represented the reviled British soldiers who had killed American colonists in the Boston Massacre. He too risked his career and reputation. These patriots, like the patriotic lawyers of the JAG, the private law firms, and the Center for Constitutional Rights, defended these hated men and women because they loved and believed in the rule of law.

Are the tribunals likely to lead to just outcomes?

The following is from a transcript of a U.S. military tribunal. The detainee, Mustafa Ait Idir, was asked to respond to a charge that he had associated with a known al-Qaeda operative while living in Bosnia.

> IDIR: Give me his name.
>
> TRIBUNAL PRESIDENT: I do not know.
>
> IDIR: How can I respond to this?
>
> TRIBUNAL PRESIDENT: Did you know of anyone that was a member of al Qaida?
>
> IDIR: No, no. . . . [T]hese are accusations that I can't even answer. . . . You tell me I am from al Qaida, but I am not al Qaida. I don't have any proof to give you except to ask you to catch Bin Laden and ask him if I am part of al Qaida. . . . What should be done is you should give me evidence regarding these accusations because I am not able to give you any evidence. I can just tell you no, and that is it.[59]

The Tribunal concluded that this man was an enemy combatant.

This is an account of Eugenia Ginzburg's trial before a Soviet Military Tribunal:

> The Military Tribunal of the Supreme Court—three officers and a secretary—faced me across a table. On either side of me were two warders. . . .

. . . I checked the time at the beginning and end of the trial. Seven minutes . . . .

"You have read the indictment?" said the president in tones of unutterable boredom. "You plead guilty? No? But the evidence shows . . ."

He leafed through a bulky file and muttered through his teeth, "For instance the witness . . . Kozlov . . ."

"Dyakonov."

"Yes. Well, they both state . . ."

But what they stated the judge was too pressed for time to read. Breaking off, he asked me:

"Any questions you wish to ask the court?"

"Yes, I do. I am accused under Section 8 of Article 58, which means that I am charged with terrorism. Will you please tell me the name of the political leader against whose life I am supposed to have plotted?"

The judges were silent for a while, taken aback by this preposterous question. They looked reproachfully at the inquisitive woman who was holding up their work. Then the one with grizzled hair muttered:

"You know, don't you, that Comrade Kirov was murdered in Leningrad?"

"Yes, but I didn't kill him. It was someone named Nikolayev. Anyway, I've never been to Leningrad. Isn't that what you call an alibi?"

"Are you a lawyer by any chance?" said the gray-haired man crossly.

"No, I'm a teacher."

"You won't get anywhere by quibbling. You may never have been in Leningrad, but it was your accomplices who killed him, and that makes you morally and criminally responsible."

In two more minutes Ginzburg, who was innocent, received a sentence: ten years in solitary confinement.[60]

American torture is now systematic. Investigative reporter Seymour M. Hersh, in his 2004 *New Yorker* essay "Torture at Abu Ghraib," showed that the torture there was not a deviation by a few psychotic privates, but a systematic policy.[61] Stephen H. Miles, M.D., also established that torture at Guantánamo was a "systematic" policy.[62]

President Bush had asked his lawyers to find the legal equivalent of "'outer space,' a 'lawless' universe," in which to keep the detainees.[63] His lawyers argued that the Geneva Convention did not apply to the prisoners. (Hitler urged his soldiers to use "unprecedented, merciless and unrelenting harshness" against Russians because "Breaches of international law by German soldiers were to be excused since Russia had not participated in the Hague Conventions and had no rights under it.")[64] Then, Guantánamo's abuses became well publicized to U.S. citizens.

That is unusual. The U.S. intelligence agents who have abused prisoners in the past have always sought to avoid scrutiny. Yet in September 2006, Bush confirmed without shame that a suspected network of secret prisons did exist worldwide.[65] Guantánamo is being built up without apologies: It was initially a $30-million-dollar construction project, but in December 2006 the Pentagon asked for $125 million to expand it further as a "permanent compound for a war-crimes court."[66]

What is this really about?

In the wake of the press frenzy over Abu Ghraib, the calm of the Bush administration was striking. Have the torturers been prosecuted—or have they been protected? To rephrase: Is it a dictatorship yet?

Of 800 subsequent investigations of primarily low-ranking U.S. soldiers, only 250 cases have resulted in any action at all; of these, there were only 89 convictions—and critics argue that the penalties in these cases have been far too soft. Only 14 members of the military out of 34 who have been suspected of causing a prisoner's death have been sentenced at all. And the toughest sentence anyone received for killing a prisoner? Five months in jail.[67] Human Rights Watch reported on July 23, 2006, that "To date, not a single military intelligence officer has been court-martialed in connection with abuse allegations in Iraq."[68] So in our secret prison system now, torturers are unlikely to be punished even when they murder people. In other words, as in the prison camps of the Gestapo and of Stalin, prisoners simply died, and that was the end of it as far as blame was concerned.

This institutional calm in the face of reports of torture, even death, suggests that the goal of establishing torture in a place beyond the rule of law may have been tactical. Americans now know a lot about how terrible the fate of a Guantánamo prisoner is.

I say again: you do not need ovens to create a fascist reality. All you need is fear. At this point, you need one highly publicized arrest of one sympathetic, non-Muslim, English-speaking Westerner caught up in the tangle of the War on Terror to be tried at Guantánamo in a publicly inadequate trial; you need one American editor or reporter or peace activist to be kept in isolation on a navy brig, unable to speak to an attorney for months. It would take one such high-profile arrest, or a mere handful of them, to chill dissent quickly in America.

We will see later how the Espionage Act, and political accusations of "espionage" and "treason," mean that we have to consider the worst-case scenarios, so we can act in time to make them impossible.

If we don't act, we are one step away from leaving the company of free democracies—nations such as the United Kingdom, France, and Sweden—and joining the ranks of such nations as Egypt, Morocco, and Pakistan.

Military Tribunals

Military tribunals are the enablers of a fascist shift.

Lenin responded to an assassination attempt by setting up secret military tribunals that bypassed the established court system.[69] Mussolini set up military tribunals to dispense summary justice. Stalin used a revived system of secretive military tribunals that also bypassed the judiciary.

The Nazis also set up a tribunal system, "People's Courts," that bypassed the formal legal system. These courts had originally been established as "an emergency body set up to dispense summary justice on looters and murderers" in 1918. These "courts" were able to sentence those charged with "treason" and were characterized by "the absence of any right of appeal against their verdicts." The "will of the people" took the place of the rule of law.[70]

When the Nazis first came to power, not only was there still an independent judiciary in Germany—there were still judges outraged at SA and SS abuses of prisoners, and human rights lawyers who shared their outrage. Earlier, one of these independent lawyers had actually sought to prosecute the SS for prisoner abuse. It was at that point that the "People's Courts" went after the lawyers, the military tribunals were strengthened, and Hitler sought legislation that retroactively protected the SS from prosecution for acts of torture.[71] (The Bush administration seeks to sheild interrogators from prosecution for war crimes.)

This too opened the door for what followed.

To push an open society closer to a closed one, leaders establish state-sanctioned torturers. In a democratic society, citizens can sue their torturers: Abner Louima, a Haitian immigrant to New York City, won nearly $9 million from the Giuliani administration and the Patrolmen's Benevolent Association after members of the police department had sodomized him with a broomstick while he was under arrest.[72] The leadership was held accountable for torture.

But in a dictatorship, the torturers and those who defend torture are placed in charge of the law. At the request of the CIA, then–legal counsel to the president Alberto Gonzales solicited the "torture memo" from the Justice Department. After the Abu Ghraib scandal, Bush did not fire Gonzales, or turn him over to authorities to face criminal charges; instead, he appointed Gonzales Attorney General of the United States of America.

The torturer was now in charge of the law.

Why torture?

It is hard to think of another policy goal that this administration has pursued with such single-minded focus as it has legalized torture. Draft memos, a Supreme Court challenge, dozens of secret meetings, and finally a full-court press to Congress: This team is trying very hard to establish a place beyond the rule of law where people can be tortured, and has effectively succeeded.

You must ask yourself: Why? Why work so hard at this?

The administration gives several explanations: Bush claims that "harsh interrogation" helps investigators gather intelligence. Law professor Alan M. Dershowitz supports the use of torture by raising the specter of a hypothetical terrorist with information about a "ticking bomb."[73] But the studies of the history of torture show that this is a practically impossible scenario. Torture makes it less likely, as military leaders and FBI interrogators confirm, that decent intelligence will come out of a prisoner's mouth. Torture is effective only at stacking up false confessions: When Chinese interrogators in the 1940s tortured U.S. prisoners of war, the Americans' "confessions" were phrased in Communist clichés.[74] As Ratner puts it, "The 'intelligence' about terrorism and terrorists that is coming out of the Guantánamo interrogations is . . . basically garbage." Many of the prisoners confessed to whatever their U.S. interrogators forced them to, because they were being denied food or medical care or simply to protect their families from the harm that U.S. interrogators threatened—as you or I would in similar circumstances.[75]

"Cooperate and you can go home," the camp's loudspeaker used to blare.

Since 2002 Bush had spearheaded a PR push for an approach—abusive treatment of prisoners—that is not that popular domestically and is horrifying to the rest of the world. Setting up a location outside the rule of law where abuse takes place seems to be one of the administration's most significant long-term goals and probably, given its performance on other fronts, one its greatest successes.

Because torturing prisoners is counterproductive if the goal is securing the Homeland, and because it makes us pariahs in the eyes of the rest of the world, then what could be some genuine reasons why this is so important to this White House?

Consider: If you have a much-hyped threat that you've used to lead the nation into war—and if case after case against the "dangerous terrorists" falls apart—don't you need false confessions? If you torture prisoners, you will certainly obtain an endless stream of false confessions. In this sense, Guantánamo is an efficient machine for producing a high-value political product: false confessions by brown people with Muslim names.

Bruce Fein of the AFA argues that the trials are for political "optics": "One might ask: Why even bother to have trials if you can hold someone forever?

"The answer I believe is political stage management: 'Because how can we demonstrate we are at war without military commissions and detainees?' "[76]

If there were a fair legal system that sorted out the guilty from the innocent, it would be impossible to maintain the main goals—not to mention the profits, though this pressure is doubtless unconscious—of the War on Terror. Too many innocent people would be sent home.

This elaborate push to torture brown people to confess to crimes they didn't commit makes political sense—even though it should make the moral sense recoil.

But why not stop at coercing Muslims? Why move on to create laws that threaten U.S. citizens themselves? Why is the language crafted by this administration now opening the door to the ability to detain and mistreat ordinary Americans who have committed no crime?

A little-noticed *New York Times* article in 2006 reported that a federal judge, Gerard E. Lynch, asked the Department of Justice attorney, Anthony J. Coppolino, if "an American lawyer who had communicated with Al-Qaeda could be grabbed on the street and interrogated about it.

"Mr. Coppolino responded, 'I would say it is possible, depending on the scenario at stake.'"[77]

As Alexander Hamilton put it in "The Federalist No. 83," "Arbitrary impeachments, arbitrary methods of prosecuting pretended offenses, and arbitrary punishments upon arbitrary convictions have ever appeared to me to be the great engines of judicial despotism."[78]

— CHAPTER FOUR —

DEVELOP *a* PARAMILITARY FORCE

A well regulated Militia, being necessary to the security of a free State, the right of the people to keep and bear Arms, shall not be infringed.

SECOND AMENDMENT

When you speak out in America, you probably feel physically safe. You don't expect that you will be intimidated physically, let alone beaten up.

In a shift toward dictatorship, though, marching and speaking out become physically scary. Often, paramilitary groups—aggressive men who have no clear, accountable relationship to the government or the party seeking power—come into play.

The Founders were driven by a vision of equality. Strong or weak, if you were counted as a citizen you had the right to speak freely. Because the Colonists had experienced abuse at the hands of the soldiers of an occupying army, the Founders set up our system to prohibit the rise of unaccountable armies on our soil. That is why the Founders gave the states the rights to establish Militias accountable only to the people. In contrast, a would-be dictator never bypasses the step—key among the ten steps—of creating a paramilitary force accountable only to himself.

I am sorry to have to tell you that a for-profit paramilitary force is being developed right now. Since 2001, as Robert Young Pelton reports in *Licensed to Kill: Hired Guns in the War on Terror,* a new kind of access to men who act like soldiers has emerged internationally, and has begun to show up at home.

The American revolutionaries fought Hessian mercenaries.

Today there is a new kind of Hessian, represented by the paramilitary forces of a company called Blackwater. Jeremy Scahill's book, *Blackwater: The Rise of the World's Most Powerful Mercenary Army*, shows how the threat from Blackwater has become ever more extreme: the firm now has

> 2,300 private soldiers deployed in nine countries, including inside the United States. It maintains a database of 21,000 former Special Forces troops, soldiers, and retired law enforcement agents on whom it can call at a moment's notice. Blackwater has a private fleet of more than twenty aircraft, including helicopter gunships and a surveillance blimp division. Its 7,000-acre headquarters in Moyock, North Carolina, is the world's largest private military facility. . . . Blackwater has more than $500 million in government contracts—and that does not include its secret "black" budget operations for U.S. intelligence agencies.

One congressman noted that in purely military terms, Blackwater could "overthrow many of the world's governments."[1] Blackwater is the world's largest private security force, works closely with Halliburton, and is available for action outside the scrutiny of Congress.

At the height of the war, there were an estimated 100,000 private contractors in Iraq, one for every U.S. soldier.[2] Blackwater paramilitary soldiers there have been reported to have shot at Iraqi civilians randomly out of cars, killing at least one, and to have harassed journalists.[3] An independent contractor for the C.I.A (not employed by Blackwater) was charged in 2006 with beating an Afghan prisoner to death.[4] But Paul Bremer's last decision as head of the Coalition Provisional Authority in Iraq was to issue "Order 17," which made private contractors such as these immune from prosecution for what would otherwise be war crimes. (Recall that the Nazis also sought laws retroactively shielding their paramilitary from prosecution for war crimes). Blackwater's lobbyists are still working hard to make sure that their men can't be prosecuted as U.S. military can: "Blackwater has openly declared its forces above the law," writes Scahill.

The company's lawyers argue that Blackwater can't be held accountable to the Pentagon's Uniform Code of Military Justice, because its soldiers are civilians. But they can't be sued in civil court either—because they are part of the U.S. military.[5]

If you think that violent dictatorship can't be directed imported to the United States, consider the case of Blackwater subcontractor Jose Miguel Pizarro Ovalle. A Chilean army officer during Pinochet's reign of terror, and a passionate Pinochet supporter, Pizarro denies the mass executions of the coup leader and claims that Bush's current and Pinochet's past missions are "exactly the same war on terror." Red Tactica, Pizarro's company, recruits former Chilean commandos to work for Blackwater: A Chilean sociologist who was tortured by Pinochet's men asserts that these recruits "are valued for their expertise in kidnapping, torturing and killing defenseless civilians." Other valued Blackwater recruits are Jordanians, Peruvians, Nigerians, and Salvadorans—all trained by countries that practice savage abuse of their civilians.[6] The president—or anyone with the cash—now has access to a paramilitary force that includes some of the world's most vicious thugs. And the president can now direct a private army of highly trained men who are not accountable to Congress—exactly one of the possibilities the Founders feared.

Blackwater is coming home, and one of our constitutional protections is at stake. The Department of Homeland Security has already begun to bring Blackwater forces to Main Street. The department paid for Blackwater soldiers to patrol the streets of New Orleans in the wake of Hurricane Katrina. According to Scahill, "By June 2006, the company had raked in some $73 million from its Katrina work for the federal government—about $240,000 a day." One unidentified private security guard said he heard "black gangbangers" shooting; the guards, armed with AR-15s and Glocks, showered bullets in the direction of the noise: "After that, all I heard was moaning and screaming, and the shooting stopped."[7]

The private security industry boomed after 9/11, because the CIA simply didn't have enough trained people to deploy in hostilities (and the National Guard was busy in Iraq). Before 2001, no U.S. firm specialized solely in trained ex-military operators. But after 9/11, firms such as Blackwater and Triple Canopy boomed, because the war "created a massive market for this type of service."[8]

The money to be made is immense. Blackwater took off with an initial $5.4 million six-month U.S. military contract. As of fall 2006, Blackwater was on track to train thirty-five thousand men over the following twelve months.[9] "Those with the money could also rent 'fire support,' complete with private gunship, intelligence gathering, aerial surveillance, armed helicopters, armored vehicles, remote-controlled blimps, and fast-attack aircraft with JDAMs (joint direct attack munitions) or cluster bombs," Pelton writes.[10]

Blackwater's business model plans increasingly to deploy its unaccountable private army in the U.S.—in the aftermath of natural disasters, and also in cases of "national emergency."

In Florida in 2000, as the disputed vote was recounted, angry mobs of young men—later identified as Republican political staffers, though they refused at the time to give their names—materialized in politically critical settings around the state, all dressed similarly, in chinos and white shirts. While the ballots were being counted and distributed in one office, one group made it clear to the officials behind the glass that they could see who was doing what.[11] Some groups of aggressive young men also congregated menacingly outside voting booths in districts in which there is a majority of African-American voters.[12] In some cases they prevented black voters from voting at all. (When, in the run-up to the Reichstag elections, the Brownshirt uniform was banned in one

German municipality, Hitler's Brownshirts simply marched in formation wearing identical white dress shirts.[13])

We have seen groups of violent, unaccountable men in America before: for instance, in the draft riots of New York City in the 19th century, the 1912 Ludlow Massacre, and Southern lynch mobs. But American mobs have not previously been disciplined, clean-cut groups such as this.

Are these random events—spontaneous meetings of young white men who shop at J. Crew and are simply quite upset about politics? Leaders who seek dictatorial power often direct a thug caste to intrude on the voting process, or to exert a sense of menace though their presence.

Mussolini was, as so often, the innovator, but both Mussolini and Hitler directed groups of aggressive young men to menace voters in or near voting booths: By 1923, a Fascist prefect in Bologna was recommending to Mussolini that members of the Fascist party should be assigned to stand "inside local polling booths, where they could act as a stimulus to responsible voting." In Ferrara, the prefects running the election went so far as to suggest that if standing in the voting booth wasn't enough, that the first voter should be beaten publicly and accused of having voted socialist—as an example to other members of the electorate.[14]

Hitler too saw the benefits of this. In 1938, William Shirer's diary recorded the "voting" that would validate Austria's annexation by Germany: "The Austrians, according to Goebbels's count, have voted ninety-nine per cent *Ja.* Maybe so. It took a brave Austrian to vote *No*, as everyone felt the Nazis had some way of checking up on how they voted. . . . There was also a wide slit in the corner of the booth which gave the election committee sitting a few feet away a pretty good view of how you voted!"[15]

Could there ever be physical intimidation in America?

The Secret Service is traditionally nonpartisan. It mission is to protect the President and other principals, not to bully Americans.

But Steven Howards, an environmental consultant from Golden, Colorado, was taking his son to a piano lesson one day in June 2006 when he saw that Vice President Cheney was appearing at a nearby mall. Howard approached his vice president and expressed his views, saying words to the effect of "I think your policies in Iraq are reprehensible." Howards continued on his way to his son's lesson. Ten minutes later, Virgil D. Reichle Jr., a Secret Service agent, handcuffed him. Agent Reichle told Howards he would be charged with "assaulting the vice president." Local police officers later filed charges against Howards that could have put him in jail for a year.

Two U.S. citizens' lawsuits charge that Secret Service or White House staff members have physically intimidated them: In 2005 three citizens—including Leslie Weise and Alex Young—were physically removed from the President's taxpayer-financed appearance in Denver for having an antiwar bumper sticker on their car in the parking lot outside. Jeff and Nicole Rank said that on Independence Day, 2004, they were arrested at a Bush appearance in Charleston, West Virginia, because they were wearing anti-Bush T-shirts.[16]

Mussolini's Thugs

Mussolini, among the dictators of his era, practically invented the strategic use of thugs: As Parliment resisted involving Italy in World War I, pro-war, proto-Fascist thugs organized street violence, attacks on newspapers, street demonstrations, and other violence. Finally, when the thugs menaced members of the political leadership themselves, Parliament caved to their wishes.[17] (Hitler picked up this intimidation scenario as well, at one point lining the halls of the working Reichstag with Brownshirts.)

By the 1922 March on Rome, Mussolini's thugs were more sophisticated and better-trained: men dressed identically in black pants and black shirts, recruited from the ranks of World War I veterans and organized into networks by Mussolini's central command. These *Arditi* did the strategic work of smashing newspaper offices, torching farmhouses, beating workers, and sexually assaulting women in the countryside. They "softened up" the population so that people were scared to resist Mussolini's forces.

Nazi Thugs

The violence of orchestrated gangs, just like their sophistication, tends to escalate over time as well. In Germany, after World War I, political parties allied themselves with armed, uniformed paramilitary groups. Their task was to march, harass members of opposing groups, and beat them—sometimes to kill them.

In 1920 the Party's paramilitary arm was founded and named the "Gymnastics and Sports Section." Their uniform was brown shirts, riding breeches, and boots. These paramilitaries roamed Munich's streets, assaulting their perceived enemies and harassing Jews. By 1921 the Free Corps, a right-wing group, was taken on board. The group was rechristened "the Storm Division," or SA, that same year. Hermann Goering led the SA by 1923. That year the storm troopers began creating a decade-long strategy of terror. These thugs would intimidate German citizens more and more directly and formally, evolving from a ragged assortment of civilians to a highly disciplined paramilitary arm of Nazi control.[18] By 1927, this thug caste was a force for the Party to direct overtly. Joseph Goebbels, now regional leader of Berlin, staged SA-led brawls in meeting-halls and in the streets. By 1929, Hitler, Goebbels, and the regional leaders of the party made a practice of hinting to the SA about what kind of violence was expected, and the SA would deliver. This strategy let the Nazi leadership remain free of legal responsibility for the violence, and it reassured middle-class law-abiding citizens that Hitler himself and his colleagues really were not to blame for this savagery.[18] The random bullies had become a parallel army.

In 1938, Nazi gangs were unleashed to wreak the chaos of *Kristallnacht*, the Night of Broken Glass: they destroyed Jewish businesses and terrified German Jews. Joseph Weinberg was a twenty-four-year-old business student from Stuttgart whose mother had run a market stall: "The next morning I went to the *Markthalle* with my mother and sister," he recounted. "When we walked upstairs, all the doors were ripped out; all the food was smashed together and lying in the center of the store and the money and everything was taken away. All we had—butter, flour, herring, everything—was piled up there. My mother, of course, cried and . . . cried. There was nothing we could do."[20]

Thugs are the advance men of every dictatorial ascendancy, and thug violence is the advance work.

In our nation's past, police action in the United States that has directed violence at citizens has backfired: Southern Civil Rights protesters in the 1960s won more public support with every image of water hoses and snarling dogs trained against them. When members of the National Guard fired on student protesters at Kent State University in 1970, killing four and wounding nine, the image helped turn the tide against the Vietnam War. There has been state violence in the United States against protesters and voters before: The possibility of it exists here just as it does in any nation.

But our laws have driven such violence back again. And we haven't had members of a mercenary army on our streets since we won our independence.

— CHAPTER FIVE —

SURVEIL ORDINARY CITIZENS

People need to watch what they say, watch what they do.
ARI FLEISCHER; former White House Press Secretary, 2001

I warn every animal on this farm to keep his eyes very wide open.
SQUEALER,
in George Orwell's *Animal Farm*

According to the ACLU's Barry Steinhardt, you should assume, if you are an activist, that your e-mail may be monitored and your phone calls tracked. He says that if your communications reach a certain level of interest to the government, a human being may be tasked to read and listen in on what you are saying and you won't know about it. The White House surveillance program is triggered by certain key words and names. (The sophisticated Stasi listening station on Brocken Mountain, which monitored ordinary citizens' calls between East and West Germany, was also programmed to record conversations when a certain name or word came up.)

Even though you pose no terrorist threat to the state, there is a reason you can be placed under surveillance now. Tyrants place populations under surveillance because this is a prime means of control. The Gestapo, the NKVD, the KGB, the Stasi, and the Chinese Politburo all requisitioned private data such as medical, banking, and library records; now, with the Internet, Chinese authorities track citizens' computer use. One reason dictators demand access to such private data is that this scrutiny breaks down citizens' sense of being able to act freely against those in power. Such intrusions also erode citizens' loyalties to civil and professional groups and redirect their primary loyalty to the state.

Torture doesn't get you better information, but the Bush team wants to be able to torture—and to let you know that torture takes place. Many critics have noted that illegal wiretapping doesn't speed intelligence gathering, but the Bush administration wants to eavesdrop on your calls and e-mails without a warrant—and to let you know that there is such surveillance underway.

Why?

The Iron Triangle in American Life

The Department of Homeland Security's surveillance apparatus is certainly aimed at prosecuting the War on Terror. But it may also be aimed at us, for domestic political purposes.

As I noted, all the societies we are looking at were facing real enemies and used surveillance to seek out their enemies. But all of them also used state surveillance against ordinary citizens to make them docile. Each dictatorship defended this on national security grounds.

In July of 2002, the Bush administration rolled out Operation TIPS, the Terrorism Information and Prevention System, which sought to recruit "a million letter carriers, meter readers, cable technicians, and other workers with access to private homes as informants to report to the Justice Department any activities they think suspicious."[1] TIPS was to begin with a pilot program in ten cities and offered citizens a toll-free number to call. The million citizens the program hoped to enlist would have worked out to one informant for every twenty-four Americans. (The ACLU notes that this pilot program alone would have doubled the Stasi's ratio of informant to citizen. In 1989, when the Stasi records were opened, the people of the former GDR were amazed to find that only a minority of citizens had actually been watched, because most had simply assumed they had open files on them.[2] That is why surveillance is effective—even cost-effective: You don't have to actually monitor citizens—just let them know they might be monitored.)

Tom Ridge, then–Secretary of the Department of Homeland Security, suggested that Americans report to the hotline about their neighbors. This trial balloon was met with mockery: Train the cable guy to spy! Though Congress soon prohibited the administration from funding TIPS, according to the ACLU, a version of the program was simply shifted to the Pentagon's "black budget." ("I don't make this stuff up," commented Steinhardt.[3])

In China, Communist officials subject citizens to three forms of government surveillance, together called the "iron triangle." (Bush referred to three of his aides as "the iron triangle.") This consists of the residence permit, which limits where you live; the secret personnel file, which records your sins and political liability; and the work unit, which supervises every aspect of your life. The *dangan,* or secret personnel file, shadows every Chinese citizen. "The *dangan* looks like a manila envelope, and there is a special postal system for transferring them around the country. If you make a serious political mistake, your leaders put a note in your *dangan*, and it will haunt you in the future whenever you try to change your job, go abroad, or get a promotion."[4]

American citizens now have a *dangan*: Three new forms of state surveillance were initiated in 2005 and 2006. *New York Times* reporters Eric Lichtblau and James Risen exposed an e-mail and phone monitoring program that was operating without legal warrants in 2005;[5] in 2006 they revealed that U.S. treasury officials, under the auspices of a CIA program, were reviewing millions of private bank transactions without individual court-ordered warrants or subpoenas.[6] The stories ran as scoops. But were these scoops undermining the government's broader agenda, or inadvertently advancing it? If you don't know you are under surveillance, you won't be intimidated. Dictatorships want citizens to know they are being watched.

The net effect of the stories, whether they were scoops or leaks (or both), was that U.S. citizens now knew that they had an "iron triangle" of surveillance over them: phone calls—social and sexual life; e-mails—work life; and bank records—financial life. Where else does one communicate private and confidential information?

Americans understand, even if most of us feel it would be only a remote possibility, that our most intimate correspondence can now be monitored by the State.

This surveillance is chilling dissent already: Emily Whitfield notes that "people are already reluctant to sign petitions. They are saying, 'I don't want my name to go on a list.'"[7]

Many citizens have noted how relatively muted Democratic and other opposition leaders seem to be in the face of all of this. The new surveillance reality helps to explain this unusual moderation in tone. Politicians understand what state surveillance means faster than ordinary people do: Political candidates assume as a matter of course that their opponents are trying to monitor them.

When I worked on the Gore 2000 campaign—working on issues of concern to women and the youth vote—staffers took it for granted that they should have sensitive conversations on landlines because cell phones were assumed to be unsecured. Before you work for the White House or for a presidential candidate, you go through a search of anything potentially embarrassing in your past or present life because everyone knows that if the opposition can find something with which to blackmail or embarrass you, they will use it. You go through your stock holdings and tax returns; review any past drug use; you have to confess to your own team any illicit affairs or mental health treatment or addiction treatment; you disclose how you pay your babysitter. You have to do this because your team needs to know what the other team can find. The National Committees devote vast amounts of money and staff time to this kind of scrutiny: it's called "opposition research," and while it's not nice, it is still playing within the rules of democracy.

But now, opposition research that used to be reserved for political leaders alone can be directed at the rest of us. Politicians are not bland and inhibited because they are naturally boring; they are bland and inhibited because they know they are being watched. So they censor themselves.

If our government's only goal were to fight terror, most

Americans would have no major problem with this kind of surveillance: They would feel that the benefit of being spared another 9/11 outweighs the discomfort of being listened in upon. Whitfield says that people often remark, "If I am not doing anything wrong, why should I worry about it?"

That faith presupposes that no one can get away with using your words or actions against you unfairly. This is a good assumption in a working democracy—but disastrous naïveté in a fascist shift.

Dictatorships use citizen surveillance in a clear way: to blackmail and coerce the people, especially critics. In the 1960s and 1970s, J. Edgar Hoover's FBI amassed files on the private lives of political, union, Civil Rights, anti-war, and other leaders, and blackmailed or harassed them. The FBI's Counter Intelligence Programs (COINTELPRO) actions against civil rights workers and the left in the 1960s included planting fake evidence on them, sending bogus letters accusing them of adultery to ruin their marriages (one fake letter called Dr. King an "evil, immoral beast" and suggested he kill himself), disclosing activists' sexually transmitted diseases, tapping their phones, getting activists fired from their jobs, distributing false articles that portrayed them as drug abusers, and planting negative articles about them in newspapers.[8]

We all have things we wish to keep private: a flirtation or even an affair, a struggle with alcohol, an old brush with the law. Think about all the things you have said in a phone conversation, sent to a friend in an e-mail, or discussed with your accountant that could, if available to someone who wanted to shut you up, be used or taken out of context to blackmail or smear you. Now understand that all of these things *are* available and *can* be used against you.

The USA PATRIOT Act set the stage for booksellers, librarians, and even doctors to have to turn over to the state information about Americans that had been private up until then. The American Booksellers Foundation for Free Expression took a stand against this and librarians spoke out as well. (National Socialists also went after the booksellers, librarians, and doctors.)

When closed societies gather information on ordinary people's lives—when people know that their book-buying and library records are open, their sexual behavior and financial decisions are no longer private, their conversations are bugged, their class lectures are taped, their protests are photographed by police, their medical records are exposed, and that all this information can be used against them—their will to challenge the regime in power falters.

Fascist and Totalitarian Surveillance

Spying is the fuel of fascism. Mussolini pioneered the use of spying as a way to control his people. After 1922, Fascists ostentatiously made lists of names of communists to be punished. By 1927, Fascists were tapping phone lines, and even spying on the Pope. Mussolini tapped his own party secretary's phone in order to blackmail him.[9] By 1933 the secret police encouraged ordinary Italians to inform on their neighbors. People were turned in for things as commonplace as singing the wrong song after they had been drinking. Secret police also tapped business leaders, including Giovanni Agnelli. Finally, Italians at every level of society understood that they were being watched.[10]

SS leader Himmler used surveillance too: He "whipped the Gestapo into an organization which . . . watches over almost every department of life in the country and which keeps for Hitler and the politicians a watchful eye on the army itself."[11] Most people in Germany did not at first support the Nazis. But as Nazis paired citizen surveillance with state violence, opposition stilled.

From 1930 onwards, the SS spied on the Brownshirts and kept files to use against them.[12] That year, police put masses of citizens under surveillance: half a million Berliners alone. Welfare officers and medical researchers began keeping lists of "asocial" citizens: Once on "the list," it was difficult to get off, and you lost jobs and benefits.[13] By the mid-1930s, most citizens understood that their conversations were no longer private, and National Socialists were bugging the conversations of reporters and political leaders. "Amusing to note of late," wrote Shirer in 1940, "on the desks of the German officials I have business with, copies of cables which I have received from, or sent to, my New York office. I of course have known for some time that they saw all my outgoing and incoming messages and have had no end of fun sending absurd messages to New York criticizing these officials by name or concocting something that would keep them guessing."[14] Amusing—if you're not subject to arrest.

Many people who lived through the Nazi years said in one survey that they had been spied on by neighbors, coworkers, fellow pupils, and police. People said that nannies, maids, office coworkers, and teachers were all enlisted as spies. As in the GDR, only a minority—between 3 and 25 in 100—were actually sure of having being spied on, but the paranoia extended to everyone.[15]

Nazi surveillance increased over the years. "You never knew who it might be when the doorbell rang," one person told the interviewers. "[W]e children were not allowed to touch the curtains. . . . There was always somebody with a leather trench coat standing there in the hallway. And, especially when there were two or three people at our place, there would be several people standing outside in front of our house."[16]

Secretary of State Condoleezza Rice is an expert on at least one surveillance society, which she analyzed in a book she co-authored, *Germany Unified and Europe Transformed*. The German film *The Lives of Others* brings this everyday Stasi surveillance to life: The playwrights assume there are bugs in their friends' apartments and discuss politics on outdoor walks; journalists assume their own apartments will be ransacked, and hide their manuscripts under floorboards. Neighbors had to inform against neighbors; students informed on professors; children were encouraged to turn in their parents. Information equaled control.

Czech authorities also used surveillance during the Cold War to crush pro-democracy agitation. Havel describes the anxiety that the Czech Secret Police cultivated as "that hideous spider whose invisible web runs right through society [causing] a dull, existential fear that seeped into every crack and crevice of daily life and made one think twice about everything one said and did."[17]

China too uses surveillance to crush democracy. Reporters Nicholas Kristof and Sheryl WuDunn, evoke a scene similar to those played out in the GDR. A Chinese friend asks Kristof to go for a walk:

> "You know Hongjun, don't you?" she asked. "Well, you should know that he's not for real. He's a spy for State Security, and you should never, ever trust him with any information. He's been a spy for a long time, and now he's interested in you and Sheryl. He's been asking about a book he thinks you're writing, and about how you're writing it. He wants to know if you're writing it on the hard drive of the computer, or on floppy disks. If you are writing a book, you might want to be very, very careful with it."

"I was speechless," writes Kristof. "I hadn't told Hongjun about a book."[18]

With these early steps in place, people start to restrict their own activities voluntarily. They start to think twice about bulk-e-mailing the "Impeach George Bush" message, or checking Amnesty International's Website to see what Iraqis with relatives held in U.S.-run prisons are saying, or sending information about the Professor Ward Churchill controversy to a friend.

In that atmosphere, dissent stifles itself before it can develop. Surveillance leads to fear and fear leads to silence.

And silence is un-American.

— CHAPTER SIX —

INFILTRATE CITIZENS' GROUPS

Congress shall make no law . . . prohibiting . . . the right of the people peaceably to assemble, and to petition the Government for a redress of grievances.

FIRST AMENDMENT

The next time you meet with your antiwar group, I am afraid you have to ask yourself if everyone present really is who you think he or she is. Incredible as it sounds, you may well have undercover investigators hanging out with you.

Dictatorships and would-be dictators routinely infiltrate legal citizen groups and report back to the group in power or seeking power. Historically, infiltrators are also directed to disrupt and harass such organizations. The goal: to make sure that it becomes too costly and nerve-wracking to act out as a citizen.

In Italy, Fascist spies infiltrated groups of trade unionists. In Stalin's Russia, spies reported on the activities of intellectuals and dissidents.[1] In Germany, National Socialist agents infiltrated groups of anti-Nazi students, Communists, and labor activists; these agents were busy, even attending cabarets where jazz and other "unGerman" music was being played, in order to denounce the musicians.[2] In the GDR, the Stasi infiltrated dissident groups of the usual targets. In Prague in 1968, infiltrators joined in with groups of writers, theatre workers, journalists, and intellectuals. In Chile, Pinochet's agents joined groups of prodemocracy students.[3] The Chinese Politburo sends state agents to infiltrate forbidden pro-democracy and banned religious groups.

Infiltration is not just an intelligence tool; like surveillance, it is also a psychological pressure point. When the state infiltrates citizen groups, people feel vulnerable about acting in accord with one another and so are less likely to risk the assertive collective behavior that democracy requires.

In dictatorships, infiltrators are joined by *agents provocateurs* at marches and rallies. These provocateurs don't just act and dress like the protesters: Their task is to provoke a violent situation or actually to commit a crime. One FBI infiltrator, Gary Thomas Rowe, for instance, warned his handler of an impending police attack on the Freedom Riders—then went ahead to participate energetically in the beatings that followed.[4] *Provocateurs* also serve a PR purpose: They set up protesters to look like lawless threats to society, thus providing would-be dictators with the rationale for declaring martial law as a means to "restore public order."

Since 2000, there has been a sharp increase in U.S. citizen groups that are being harassed and infiltrated by police and federal agents, often in illegal ways. A 2006 ACLU report notes that police departments in California had infiltrated antiwar protests, political rallies, and other constitutionally protected gatherings and were secretly investigating them, even though the California state constitution forbids this.[5]

But that was just the beginning. A Defense Department program called Talon created a database of "anti-terror" information about peaceful U.S. citizen groups and activists.[6] Talon included details of antiwar groups' planning meetings in churches; a church service for peace in New York City; even details of the meetings of such all-American groups as Veterans for Peace. The Defense Department even had e-mails that had been forwarded to it by people who had pretended to be members of the groups.[7] Some of the groups were placed in this database with the rationale that while they weren't violent yet, they might become so. Jen Nessel of the Center for Constitutional Rights said, "We have absolutely moved over into a preventive detention model—you look like you could do something bad, you might do something bad, so we're going to hold you."[8]

Harassment is a more serious tactic. Before the Republican convention in New York in 2004, the police department's intelligence team sent detectives throughout the city to infiltrate groups planning to demonstrate peacefully at the convention. When the New York Civil Liberties Union asked to unseal the records of this undercover spying, lawyers for the city argued that the records should be kept secret, because the news media would "fixate upon and sensationalize them."[9]

It is in a fascist shift that the truth is recategorized as being unseemly—destructively inflammatory.

Today, if you are outspoken, you are increasingly likely to face other kinds of harassment, such as an IRS investigation: All Saints Episcopal Church in Pasadena, California, was scrutizined by the IRS after a rector gave a sermon that characterized Jesus as antiwar. (A year after the 1917 Espionage Act was passed, Rev. Clarence Waldron was sentenced to prison for fifteen years for passing out a pamphlet that said that war was un-Christian.[10])

The IRS asked for the California church's internal documents and e-mails in order to investigate if it had violated tax law.[11] Many conservative churches have helped Republicans: Two Ohio churches turned their facilities over to Republican groups, hosted Republican candidates, and were credited with turning out voters for Bush in 2004. But they were not investigated by the IRS.[12]

Harassment takes many forms: Peace activist Cindy Sheehan wore a T-shirt with the message, "2,245 Dead. How many more?" referring to the war in Iraq, in the gallery of the House of Representatives. Capitol Police arrested her and charged her with "unlawful conduct," which could have given her a year in prison. Beverly Young, a Republican congressman's wife, wore a T-shirt in the same place that read, "Support Our Troops"; she was asked to leave, but was not arrested or charged with a crime.[13]

On July 25, 2006, Jim Bensman, a coordinator with Heartwood, an environmental organization, was at a public meeting in Illinois convened by the Army Corps of Engineers to discuss proposed construction of a channel on a dam in the Mississippi River. Bensman advocated a standard solution to the problem under discussion: using explosives. Dams are typically destroyed with explosives, a point which the Corps of Engineers' own presentation at the meeting noted. News coverage of the meeting included the summary that Bensman "would like to see the dam blown up."

Less than a week later, Bensman got called an FBI agent. The agent persuaded him that the call was for real by telling Bensman about items in his FBI file. The agent also told Bensman that he wanted to visit him at home. Bensman recalls: "I was thinking, 'I need to talk to an attorney'. . . and he said, 'Well, O.K., I will put you down as not cooperating.' "[14]

So Americans do need to watch what they say, watch what they do. Be careful how you phrase things. Don't leave your meeting's minutes lying around. Check your gut reaction when you are talking to people in your local group. Be mindful while you pursue your activism.

Have the number of a good lawyer handy.

But most important of all, lead your friends and community to unite in a grassroots movement to restore our nation's freedom.

— CHAPTER SEVEN —

ARBITRARILY DETAIN *and* RELEASE CITIZENS

The Press Department of the Foreign Ministry judged that . . . I was urging the "spread of counterrevolutionary developments in the GDR." Because of the role I was clearly playing "in the ideological war of imperialist media against the GDR" I should be placed on the list . . .

TIMOTHY GARTON ASH

Protest has been lively in our nation throughout most of our history because being free means that you can't be detained arbitrarily. We have also felt free in the security of our homes, believing that the state can't break in and go through our possessions.

All that is changing.

"THE LIST"

In 2002, I began to notice that almost every time I sought to board a domestic airline flight, I was called aside by the Transportation Security Administration and given a more thorough search. When this was happening on nine flights out of ten, I asked the officials about the special search. They told me that the search was due to the quadruple "S" that routinely came up on my boarding pass. There are several reasons why one might receive a quadruple "S" on one's boarding pass if one doesn't fit a terrorist profile: buying a ticket at the last minute, for instance, or paying in cash. But those circumstances didn't apply to me. I kept asking, but not getting real answers.

This stepped-up search became so routine as I traveled that companions who were flying with me began to simply say, "I'll meet you at the gate," even before we got through the security line.

On yet another preboarding search, I asked yet again. The TSA agent searching me, a young woman, said pleasantly, "You're on the list."

"The *list*?" I asked. "What list?" Her supervisor abruptly ended our exchange, took over from her, and then moved me on.

Indeed, the TSA Administration does keep a "list." The American citizens on the list who do not fit a terrorist profile range from journalists and academics who have criticized the White House to activists and even political leaders who have also spoken out.

These TSA searches and releases would be trivial in a working democracy. In the 1960s, peace activists found it merely irksome to be trailed by FBI agents, and in the 1980s those who organized The Committee in Solidarity with the People of El Salvador (CISPES) on college campuses were even amused sometimes to find, on submitting a Freedom of Information Act request, that there was a file open on them. But once the first steps in a fascist shift are in place, being on "the list" is not really funny any more.

When you are physically detained by armed agents because of something that you said or wrote, it has an impact. On the one hand, during these heightened searches of my luggage, I knew I was a very small fish in a very big pond. On the other hand, you get it right away that the state is tracking your journeys, can redirect you physically, and can have armed men and women, who may or may not answer your questions, search and release you.

Our faith in nonarbitrary "safe" detention helps to make us Americans. When I was twenty, I joined a group of graduate students who traveled from Oxford to London—to get arrested. We all went over to the American embassy: There we sat, self-consciously, on the chilly concrete steps, with our "U.S. OUT OF EL SALVADOR" banner unfurled on our knees. A police van arrived.

Bored British police officers took us away. We were locked up for a few hours and then, of course, released.

"Silly season," one of the bobbies commented civilly as he signed the paperwork that let us go. I wasn't scared to speak out because I was in a democracy and the rule of law protected me.

That kind of experience of accountable detention and release is eroding in America. Activists are not being beaten. But they are being watched, and sometimes intimidatingly detained and released.

In America, people are not supposed to be detained because of their political beliefs. But Senator Edward M. "Ted" Kennedy, the liberal senator from Massachusetts who is a thorn in the side of the Bush administration, was detained five times in East Coast airports in March, 2004. Democratic Congressman John Lewis of Georgia has also been subjected to extra security measures.[1]

On September 21, 2004, U.S. security officials diverted to Bangor, Maine, a United Airlines flight from London to Washington D.C. On board was Usef Islam, once known as the singer Cat Stevens. Customs and Border Protection agents questioned him on "national security grounds."[2] Most Americans associate Cat Stevens not with bomb-building in al-Qaeda training camps, but with slow-dancing to "Wild World" in suburban rec rooms. Islam's detention helps "blur the line"—he is "one of us."

Jan Adams and Rebecca Gordon, American peace activists, tried to check in at the San Francisco airport for a trip to Boston in August 2002. Airport personnel who said that these middle-aged women were on the "master list" called the police and notified the FBI. At least twenty other peace activists are confirmed to be on the list: A 74-year-old Catholic nun who works for peace was detained in Milwaukee; Nancy Oden, a leader of the Green Party, was prevented from flying from Maine to Chicago.[3] Free speech advocates are on the list: King Downing of the ACLU was detained in the Boston airport in 2003.[4] David Fathi, also of the ACLU, was detained as well.[5] Scholars who defend the Constitution are on the list: in 2007, Professor Walter F. Murphy, emeritus of Princeton, one of the nation's foremost Constitutional scholars, who had recently spoken critically of Bush's assault on the Constitution, was detained for being on a "watch list." A TSA official confirmed informally that it was probably because Murphy had criticized the President, and warned him that his luggage would be ransacked.[6]

In 2005, "Evo Morales"—which is the name of the President of Bolivia, who has criticized Bush—appeared on the list, beside President Morales' birthdate.[7] After Hugo Chavez, the President of Venezuela, gave a speech at the United Nations criticizing Bush, Chavez's foreign minister, Nicolas Maduro, was detained at Kennedy Airport. When Maduro explained that he was Venezuela's foreign minister, he said that officers "threatened and shoved" him. According to President Chavez, the officers accused Maduro of participating in terrorist acts.[8] The chilling effect from this last example could be profound: Any staffer of any foreign government or international regulatory body can be detained.

Now, there are tens of thousands of people on the list.[9]

Where did the list come from? In 2003, President Bush had the intelligence agencies and the FBI create a "watch list" of people thought to have terrorist intentions or contacts. These agencies gave the list to the TSA and the commercial airlines. *60 Minutes* got one copy of the list: It was 540 pages long. That list of people to be taken aside for extra screening had 75,000 names on it. The more stringent "no-fly list" had 45,000 names; before 9/11 there were just 16 names. The list is so secret that even Congresspeople have been prevented from looking at it. People on the list endure searches that can last for hours. One American citizen, Robert Johnson, described "the humiliation factor" of being strip-searched: "I had to take off my pants. I had to take off my sneakers, then I had to take off my socks. I was treated like a criminal." Donna Bucella, who was at that time head of the FBI program that oversaw the list, told *60 Minutes*, "Well, Robert Johnson will never get off the list."[10]

On December 6, 2006, Democrats in Congress tried to find out more about recent reports that the Department of Homeland Security "was using a scoring system" that rated the dangers posed by people crossing American borders. The Democrats were worried that these lists did not simply keep people from flying—they could keep them from getting jobs as well. According to the *New York Times*, Vermont Senator Patrick J. Leahy said that "the program and broader government data-mining efforts could make it more difficult for innocent Americans to travel or to get a job—without giving them the chance to know why they were labeled a security risk."[11] So now there is not just the anxiety that you might be detained—you could also, if you are on certain secret lists, be turned down for a job and never know why.

Being on the list can get also get some people detained and tortured—although they are innocent.

Maher Arar is a Canadian citizen, a software consultant, husband, and father—a North American yuppie. The United States detained Arar when he was changing planes at Kennedy Airport in 2002. He was "rendered" to Syria. Security forces there kept him in prison for over a year, beating him repeatedly with a heavy metal cable. The Canadian government pursued a two-year investigation and concluded that it had all been a terrible mistake—Arar actually had no ties to terrorists whatsoever. Canadians were so appalled by this miscarriage of justice that the head of the Royal Canadian Mounted Police resigned. After he was released with his government's help, Arar, emboldened perhaps by living in a working North American democracy, sued the U.S. government.

The Bush administration refused to concede that it had been wrong; refused to provide documents or witnesses to the Canadian investigators; and finally announced in January 2007 that they had "secret information" that justified keeping Arar on the list.[12]

So Arar, a North American citizen like you or me, has to live in fear, perhaps for the rest of his life (his CCR lawyer says he suffers from post-traumatic stress): Arar turns down offers to receive honors overseas, for whenever he travels—if he dares to—over borders, he fears being taken off the plane or train, shipped to another country and subjected to torture *again*.

Making it more difficult for people out of favor with the state to travel back and forth across borders is a classic part of the fascist playbook. As Nazi Germany closed down, borders tightened and families fleeing internment were traumatized by the uncertainties that they knew they faced at the borders. When reporter Timothy Garton Ash published essays that offended the Stasi, he was forbidden to re-enter the GDR. The United States has recently been refusing visas to various respected Muslim scholars from universities such as Oxford—scholars with no ties whatsoever to terrorists—because they have been critical of U.S. policy. This has happened before in America: in the 1950s the FBI confiscated the passports of intellectuals and journalists who had been critical of anticommunist witch hunts.[13]

William Shirer described the tension of airport searches of suspect individuals—reporters—in Berlin in 1938:

> Hans Kaltenborn, our star foreign news commentator, was turned back by the secret police when he arrived at Tempelhof [airport] from London this afternoon. . . . I became suspicious when the passport officials continued to hold him after all the other passengers had been cleared. . . . [Kaltenborn's] German relatives, who were exposing themselves to possible arrest by merely being there, remained bravely at the rail. I finally complained to a Gestapo man about keeping us standing so long. . . . [A] Gestapo officer came up and announced that Hans would be taking the six o'clock plane back to London.
>
> "Why, he's just come from there," I spoke up.
>
> "And he's returning there now," the officer said.
>
> "May I ask why?" Hans said, boiling inside but cool outside, though beads of sweat bubbled out on his forehead.
>
> The officer had a ready answer: Looking in his note-

> book, he said with tremendous seriousness: "Herr Kaltenborn, on such and such a date in Oklahoma City, you made a speech insulting the Führer."
>
> "Let me see the text of that, please," Hans spoke up. But you do not argue with the Gestapo. . . . Hans was hustled out. . . . Then he disappeared.[14]

Are the cases we hear of Americans being caught up in detention, searches, and releases merely Homeland Security or TSA zealotry? Or are the stories effective PR about a new reality? Fascist propagandists target individuals, detain and release them, and then publicize the stories. Could all these—Bensman the fish defender and Cat Stevens the balladeer and the little elderly nun and the lady peace activists—be victims *not* of simple clumsiness but, rather, examples of the fact that perfectly ordinary Americans can now get entangled in the increasingly punitive apparatus of the state?

Could what happened to Maher Arar happen to a U.S. citizen? Chaplain James Yee was arrested and investigated on suspicion of "espionage and possibly treason" on September 10, 2003. It is not widely reported that he had also spoken up on behalf of better treatment for the detainees in Guantánamo. Military officials claimed that Yee had classified documents that included diagrams of cells at Guantánamo and lists of detainees. He was also said to have "ties to [radical Muslims in the U.S.]."

Chaplain Yee was taken to a navy brig in Charleston, South Carolina, and interrogated.[15] He was blindfolded; his ears were blocked; he was manacled and then put into solitary confinement for seventy-six days; forbidden mail, television, or anything to read except the Koran. His family was not allowed to visit him. He was demonized on TV, radio, and the Internet and accused of being an operative in "a supposed spy ring that aimed to pass secrets to al-Qaeda from suspected terrorists held at Guantánamo. . . . Court papers said he would be charged with espionage, spying, aiding the enemy, mutiny or sedition, and disobeying an order." Chaplain Yee, born in New Jersey and raised a Lutheran before he converted to Islam, was baffled at the accusations. His lawyers were told he could face execution. Within six months, the U.S. government had dropped all criminal charges against Yee. But the government said it did so to avoid making its sensitive evidence public, not because Yee is innocent.

Yee was released—but charged with what looked like punitive "Mickey Mouse" charges: "adultery, lying to investigators and two counts of downloading porn." In the presence of his humiliated wife and his four-year-old daughter, military prosecutors compelled Navy Lt . Karyn Wallace to testify about their extramarital affair. The military rarely prosecutes adultery. The government never presented the evidence on which it based its first accusations against Yee. But after Yee was set free, he was placed "under a new Army order not to talk about his ordeal in any way that might be seen as critical to the military." If he says anything negative about what happened to him, he faces further prosecution.[16]

(In 2007, Lieutenant Colonel William H. Steele, who like Chaplain Yee has spoken up for a more humane situation for the detainees, would also find himself accused of "aiding the enemy," for various charges, and facing possible execution.[17])

So in Yee's case a United States citizen innocent of the initial charges was kept in solitary confinement, this time for 76 days. His name was destroyed, his family humiliated—*and he can't talk about it or he will be arrested again.*

On July 24, 2006, Chaplain Yee said he had been detained once again, this time at the Canadian border as he was trying to come home after a trip to Vancouver to see a performance. Yee was questioned for two hours.[18] You can imagine how that "Come with us" might have felt.

In Germany, by 1933, arbitrary arrest and release was common. On November, 27, 1938, two police officers came to Victor Klemperer's house to search for weapons. As they ransacked the possessions of the two middle-aged German Jews, Mrs. Klemperer made the mistake of asking them not to go through the linen cupboard with unwashed hands. Professor Klemperer was taken into custody and released: "[A]t four o'clock I was on the street with the curious feeling, free—but for how long?" (In 1941, Klemperer would spend eight days in prison for forgetting to close the curtains on his windows for the blackout.)

The charges against those taken into custody and then released were often vague and uncontestable. In a survey of German citizens who had lived through that era, 36 percent reported having been arrested, questioned, and released. A well-known Cologne priest who was outspoken about the Nazis was arrested and released repeatedly.[19] As the 1930s progressed hundreds of thousands of German citizens were arbitrarily detained and released.[20]

General Pinochet used this tactic too: Every so often the military would enter a slum, arrest people in random sweeps, keep them behind bars briefly, and then let them go. The only real reason was to intimidate the population.[21]

"Arbitrary Search and Seizure"

> *The right of the people to be secure in their persons, houses, papers, and effects, against unreasonable searches and seizures, shall not be violated, and no Warrants shall issue, but upon probable cause, supported by Oath or affirmation, and particularly describing the place to be searched, and the persons or things to be seized.*
>
> The Fourth Amendment

You've heard the phrase "unreasonable searches and seizures," and like so much about the Bill of Rights, in a time when democracy has been subcontracted out to lawyers and activists, it is hard for ordinary people to understand what the urgency of this could be. If you don't know the history of tyranny out of which our nation was formed, this arcane language, which no one puts in context for you, can almost sound like an unimportant scolding to "play fair"—like a parent insisting that your brother not go through your things without permission. What's the big deal about "unreasonable search and seizure"?

The FBI accused Brandon Mayfield, another ordinary yuppie—an American lawyer from Portland, Oregon—of supporting terrorism. They asserted that it was his fingerprints on evidence from the bombings in Madrid. Agents secretly broke into his house and law office and seized his computer. Mayfield, a convert to Islam, has a wife and children. You can imagine the feeling of coming home with your kids to find that strangers have broken in and been through your—and their—possessions.

You probably heard the saturation news coverage that implied that Mayfield was involved with terrorism. It turned out that Mayfield was innocent. But even when the Spanish government protested that his fingerprints did not match the prints from the bombings, the United States—again—refused to acknowledge the mistake and jailed Mayfield for two weeks in 2004, including time in solitary confinement and the prison's mental ward.[22] The charges were eventually dropped. (In November 2006 the U.S. government agreed to pay Mayfield two million dollars to settle a lawsuit challenging the constitutionality of the USA PATRIOT act which the FBI had used to obtain his personal records.[23])

Most of us don't fully understand the details of the debate over the Bush administration's efforts to avoid getting a legal warrant for each time that it reads our e-mails, opens our mail, and listens in on our phone calls—or enters our homes unbeknownst to us. President Bush wants to get, effectively, a "blanket warrant" to do these things. Many of us might think that "a blanket warrant" sounds reasonable, even efficient, in a time of war.

The Founders knew how scary a blanket warrant was, in war or peace. The Fourth Amendment specifically rejects vague general warrants.

Why? Because colonial Americans knew firsthand how abusively authorities could use the power of a blanket warrant to break into their homes and seize their private papers. General warrants had let officers of the British crown violate the privacy of colonial American homes and businesses again and again. The British Crown taxed everything from stoves to soap to papers, from candles to glass to, of course, tea. At that time, customs agents of the Crown would violently break into people's homes, rip up their trunks and cabinets, loot their papers, and haul off their goods—even if they weren't hiding anything that they should have paid taxes on.

Colonial pamphleteers in 1754 warned of the danger of these agents having the power to destroy doors, break open locks, bolts, and chains, and invade people's bedrooms and cellars armed with no more than a general warrant. A general warrant meant that these agents could go wherever they wanted without having to show a magistrate that there was a reason for their suspicion that a certain person was breaking the law. It meant that no one's home was ever truly private or safe.[24] Because of these violations of their homes, drafters of the Constitution created the Fourth Amendment.

It is tyrants and dictators who send agents to break into people's homes and offices, to seize their papers, and destroy their goods.

Curtailing Citizens' Assembly

If there is a march for, say, the Constitution, we expect to be able to get on a bus, or take a subway, and join our assembled fellow citizens. Every pro-democracy movement depends on people being willing and able to march as a mass; the sheer numbers of citizens is one of a budding or threatened democracy's most potent weapons. It is masses of people united who brought down the Berlin Wall; stood up to Chinese tanks; and overwhelmed a dictator in the Philippines. Massed citizens ended Jim Crow laws and brought the war in Vietnam to a close. It is so simple a tool, but so powerful.

This is why a dictatorship restricts the movements and assembly of its citizens—usually through municipal ordinances and curfews: Mussolini's *arditi*, for instance, warned Italian citizens to stay indoors during the fascists' mass rallies. In Mexico, police shot at and wounded student protesters in 1968.[25] General Pinochet's forces also fired at protesters in 1982.[26] Suppression of protests habituates citizens to the idea that the state has the right to direct their movements and to disperse large groups or to keep them from gathering in the first place.

In America, citizens are supposed to have the right "peaceably to assemble." But in 2004, during the Republican National Convention, New York City officials denied demonstrators access to the Great Lawn in Central Park. Mayor Michel Bloomberg's administration denied that politics had played a role in banning the demonstration. But the National Council of Arab Americans and the ANSWER Coalition, an antiwar group, brought suit. E-mails revealed that while Bloomberg's aides gave the rationale of "security" for denying the permit, the true reasons were political: "It is very important that we do not permit any big or political events for the period between Aug. 23 and Sept. 6, 2004," read one Parks Department e-mail.[27]

In New York, that wasn't the end of the pressure against free assembly. In August of 2006, the New York Police Department sought new rules that made it illegal for groups of more than 35 people to gather for sidewalk marches without a permit. The NYCLU pointed out that this proposal would have restricted a wide range of citizens' daily group activities, such as school field trips and funeral processions: "A couple jaywalking or a family riding bicycles without stopping at every red light would be subject to arrest for parading without a permit," the NYCLU wrote in an op-ed in the *Times*.[28]

For now, U.S. citizens can still assemble, march, and make their voices heard. You must ally with the many Independents and

Republicans around you who love their country and cherish these rights—don't just talk to your like-minded friends. We must practice our rights now while our voices can still carry—raising them together in defense of freedom.

— CHAPTER EIGHT —

TARGET KEY INDIVIDUALS

No one can equate the consequences for those who are spied on. (In East Germany: loss of university place, like Young Brecht; loss of job, like Erhard Haufe; reprisals against your children, as happened to Werner, and imprisonment, as in the case of Dr. Warmbier, with the court's sentence decided in advance—by the prosecution.)

TIMOTHY GARTON ASH

All dictatorships and would-be dictators strategically target key individuals. Job loss or career setbacks are the first kinds of pressure these people are likely to face.

In 2001, the National Science Foundation made it clear that its grants would no longer go to research on the basis of the science alone if that research undermined the Bush administration's agenda. If a researcher's grant sources are closed down, he or she is neutered as a scientist. The Bush administration has stacked scientific advisory committees, which are not supposed to be political, with partisans. In February of 2004, the Union of Concerned Scientists issued a condemnation of these abuses, signed by 6,000 scientists.[1]

Again, this pressure is not an original idea. Goebbels purged the sciences as well—even setting up an institute for race-based science to replace the degenerate science-based science of non-"coordinated" reality. When German scientists complained that scientific enquiry was suffering because their ranks had been purged of those who did not agree with the "party line," Hitler remarked that in his view Germany could get along without physics or chemistry for a hundred years.[2]

Universities keep alight the campfires of free speech, so it's not surprising that Bush supporters seems have a strategy to target critics on campus. In California, a bill called SB5, the "Student Bill of Rights," seeks legally to "balance" classroom discussion. David Horowitz, of the well-funded right-wing Center for the Study of Popular Culture, drafted a model of this law. His version has found supporters in Congress. (On May 1, 1933, the *Neue Studentenrecht* law was passed in Germany, aimed at using student organizations to align universities with the values of the National Socialist state.)[3]

Campus Republicans, helping their Senator introduce SB5, said "certain instructors at SRJC (Santa Rosa Junior College) are in violation of California State Law." On February 24, 2005, someone posted bright red stars on the doors of ten left-wing faculty members at that college—a state-funded institution.[4]

State legislators in the United States are putting pressure on regents to put pressure on academics who criticize the Bush agenda—another tactic with historical antecedents. Professor Ward L. Churchill was a tenured professor of Ethnic Studies at the University of Colorado. He wrote an essay that argued metaphorically that many of the 9/11 victims were not "innocent." Ill-timed? Callous? Certainly. But in an open society, hearing offensive language is the price we pay for open debate.

A group of alumni supportive of the Bush administration called on the Board of the University of Colorado to take action against Churchill. Republican state legislators added their pressure. The state legislature oversees the Board of Regents, and the Board of Regents oversees the President of the University of Colorado.[5] In June 2006, Professor Churchill, who has tenure—which means they pretty much can't fire you—was accused of "academic misconduct." His lawyer says the real reason is his political speech.[6]

In 2006, Kevin Barrett, a lecturer on Islam at the University of Wisconsin—another state school—was at the center of a similar firestorm. Barrett has "disputed official findings on the perpetrators of the Sept 11 attacks," though a University review established that he had not discussed his personal views in the classroom.

But conservative talk radio attacked Barrett, and Wisconsin

Republicans in the legislature asked for action: "Republican Representative Stephen Nass announced: 'Barrett has to go.'" Representative Nass used the strategy that had worked in Colorado. Sixty-one Wisconsin state legislators—60 of them Republicans—condemned Barrett's "academically dishonest views" and asked that he be fired. The resolution was sent to university officials. The University of Wisconsin is a state institution like Churchill's university (and Klemperer's own Dresden Technical University, where he had been Chair of Romance Languages and a Montesquieu scholar, before he was fired). Provost Patrick V. Farrell, whose own budget and salary is determined by the state legislature, tried to resist the pressure: "I want to avoid as much as we can creating some kind of political test for instructors or faculty," he said.[7]

In times of pressure, citizens can soon tell "which way the wind is blowing." Individuals realign themselves and their views. Shortly after this furor, Stanley Fish, now a professor of law at Florida International University, wrote an op-ed for *The New York Times* that argued that professors who introduce partisan ideas in their lectures deserve to be fired. Academic freedom, he wrote, does not include the right to express such views in the classroom.[8] (Martin Heidegger wrote an essay in 1933, "The Self-Assertion of the German University." Supporting Nazi views of purpose of the academy, Heidegger argued that "academic freedom" was a passé notion that should be expelled from the German university.[9])

Ideally, professors shouldn't advocate directly to students in the classroom. But in the atmosphere of self-censorship that Fish was defending, a professor could get in trouble for teaching the history of the Bush administration's failure to sign accords to stem global warming, or the history of the Constitution in light of recent events. Professors of political science, journalism, economics, and Constitutional law are in special jeopardy: There is no way to advance a discussion about these live issues without stumbling upon an observation that could be construed as "a political opinion."

Whether driven by Mussolini or by Goebbels, by Pinochet or

by China's Politburo, it's always the same tactic: The state leans on university administrators, who lean on professors and students.

Italian Fascists leaned on university rectors to scrutinize the politics of those whom they oversaw: The rector of Milan's Catholic University actively informed on politically anti-Fascist students to the secret police. If you were either a student or a professor in Mussolini's Italy, expressing unpopular views could get you fired—or even arrested and sent to internal exile. By 1927, if you wanted to secure welfare benefits or get a job or a promotion, citizens, including academics, faced a political litmus test.[10]

Germany emulated the tactic: From the early 1930s, professional purges led so many Jewish and "communist" academics and scientists to emigrate that this led to a major brain drain. By 1933, about 2,000 of the nation's premier artists and writers had fled as well.[11] The Nazi periodical *The Nettle* depicted this emigration as "a triumph for the German nation."[12]

The National Socialist German Students' League was set up in 1926. It sought to get independent professors fired and to direct the universities' resources toward Nazi goals rather than toward pure research. By 1933, Propaganda Minister Goebbels set in motion one of these purges: "By the beginning of the academic year 1933–34, 313 full professors had been dismissed. . . . By 1934, some 1600 out of 5000 university teachers had been forced out of their jobs. . . . Very quickly, newly Nazified Education Ministries made political criteria central not only for appointments but also for teaching and research."[13] On May 10, 1933, pro-Nazi students also orchestrated a series of book burnings—events designed to look "spontaneous" but actually directed behind the scenes by Goebbels.[14]

This pressure on students and academics worked in Chile in the early 1970s as well. Chilean students had been among the few who still dared to march, hold meetings, pass out flyers, and create posters attacking Pinochet after his military coup. But Pinochet purged nonaligned academics and university administrators and put his own military officers in those positions. He closed down whole departments, gutted some university programs, and moved others to new locations. He made it clear that student life was now under new management: that of his cronies. It was obvious to Chilean academics that they had to support the Junta or give up their careers.[15]

Students and academics are always democracy's foot soldiers: Czech students helped bring about the Prague Spring democracy movement. Students in Shanghai and Beijing led the democracy movement in 1989: It was Chinese art students who set up the stature of Lady Liberty in Tiananmen Square.

You may not get hurt if you are a prodemocracy student in a violent dictatorship, but you can become unemployable: Tang Rimei, an advocate of the Tiananmen democracy movement at her university, fled arrest. When she returned to her university, her professors begged the state police not to arrest her: They protected her by promising to punish her administratively. Tang was grateful: "That meant I was able to stay at the university and graduate . . . [but] I couldn't get a job."[16]

Pressure on Artists and Entertainers

The Bush administration and its supporters use economic pressure to silence or punish another group of the "usual suspects" who are always targeted in a fascist shift: artists and entertainers. In 2001, *Politically Incorrect* host Bill Maher said the 9/11 hijackers were "not cowards." Right-wing media drove a volley of criticism. Maher's advertisers, major corporations such as Sears, withdrew their support of the show. ABC cancelled the show when the season ended.

During a London concert on the eve of the Iraq war, Natalie Maines, the Dixie Chicks' lead singer, said that "We're ashamed the president of the United States is from Texas." Right-wing bloggers attacked the group: the highly organized blog Freerepublic.com called for a consumer boycott. By the end of the week there was a 20 percent decline in the airplay of their songs.[17] Cumulus Media, which owns 262 stations, stopped 42 of its stations from playing their music. Their manager said the boycott was not spontaneous but organized. *The New York Times* reported in 2006 that other recording artists were scared to express views critical of the Bush administration—out of fear of being "Dixie Chicked."[18]

A Cumulus station in Shreveport, Louisiana, held an event that included a bulldozer crushing the Dixie Chicks' CDs.[19] As I mentioned earlier, other "spontaneous" groups burned the CDs. The band is back in favor—now with different fans—and even winning Grammys; but the lesson of what can happen to an artist remains.

In 2007, the Bush administration even threatened action against filmmaker Michael Moore, raising questions about whether it would confiscate his new film *Sicko* before it had a chance to be released in theaters.[20]

Goebbels understood well the power of image to shape opinion, and thus the need to control all aspects of communications and culture: In 1933, he set up separate departments to Nazify "propaganda, radio, the press, film, theatre, and popular enlightenment."[21] Cabaret singers, actors, directors, and musicians who would not "co-ordinate" with the regime were closed down professionally. Those who did support it often saw their careers thrive.

Czech arts saw a similar freeze in 1948. But two decades later, Czech theater, writing, cartooning, and visual arts sprang back to life during the Prague Spring. This explosion was seen as destabilizing: The government cracked down once again. Finally, only "official" art, music, writing, and theatre was left unthreatened. General Pinochet also went after artists and performers: One of the first people to be "disappeared" in the coup was the beloved folk singer Victor Jara.[22] (Castro's Cuba and Somoza's Nicaragua jailed artists, writers, and performers too. The creative voice is dangerous to dictators of any persuasion.) In the 1950s, McCarthy's supporters in

Congress threatened movie studios heads with boycotts unless they in turn pressured their actors, producers, and screenwriters to cooperate with the Senate hearings. Those who still refused to comply were blacklisted by major media outlets such as CBS and Hearst, and found it difficult to work.[23]

Pressure on Civil Servants

In a fascist shift, while entertainers are the most visible, civil servants are the most vulnerable to being targeted with job loss: They work directly for the leadership. Goebbels, as we saw, purged the civil service in 1933, and private industries followed suit. He directed special ire at lawyers and judges.

Victor Klemperer writes of a senior district attorney at the High Court in Berlin who was not a Party member. The government fired him, calling the move "temporary retirement." Independent district attorneys across the nation were purged as well, and replaced by lawyers who were loyal to the regime.[24]

The Bush administration has purged civil servants who do not follow the "party line," long before the United States Attorneys scandal. When *Washington Post* reporter Dana Priest exposed the secret CIA prisons, the Bush White House fired the civil servant who leaked the information.[25] The Justice Department also let it be known that it was opening a criminal investigation into the leak of information to the *New York Times* about the NSA eavesdropping program.[26]

In 2003, Lt. Commander Charles D. Swift was assigned to represent Salim Hamdan, a 26-year-old Yemeni taxi driver accused of having been a driver for bin Laden. The Bush administration wanted the military lawyer to get his client to plead guilty. Swift was appalled that his client's access to a lawyer was dependent on his willingness to have him negotiate a "guilty" plea.[27] You can't go along with that, if you are a lawyer in America: You have taken an oath to represent your client for real. "Instead of carrying out this morally repugnant task," noted the *New York Times*, "Commander Swift concluded that the commissions were unconstitutional. He did his duty and defended his client. . . . The Navy responded by killing his military career." This sent a message to all the other military attorneys about what they risked if they refused to sell out their clients.[28]

Private lawyers who helped detainees were also threatened with career hits: In January 2007, Charles Stimson, Deputy Assistant Secretary of Defense for Detainee Affairs, expressed "shock" that American law firms would represent the detainees, and suggested that companies refuse to do business with them—in essence, a boycott. He read out a list of the names of those very law firms on a radio station.[29] A boycott could cripple those firms. (Senior Nazis orchestrated an economic boycott of Jewish-owned law firms, among other boycotted businesses. Germans who were legally represented by Jews or who shopped at Jewish-owned firms were "traitors.") These boycotts not only destroyed Jews economically years before "the final solution": they also created a "no-go zone" in which ordinary Germans understood that if they spoke up for the "others" they, too, would face reprisals.

If you can show citizens that they can lose their livelihood if they refuse to comply with the party line, it doesn't take long to "co-ordinate" an intimidated civil society.

— CHAPTER NINE —

RESTRICT *the* PRESS

Congress shall make no law respecting an establishment of religion, or prohibiting the free exercise thereof; or abridging the freedom of speech, or of the press . . .

First Amendment

In all dictatorships, targeting the free press begins with political pressure—loud, angry campaigns for the news to be represented in a way that supports the group that seeks dominance. Attacks escalate to smears, designed to shame members of the press personally; then editors face pressure to fire journalists who are not parroting the party line. A caste of journalists and editors who support the regime develops, whether out of conviction, a wish for advancement, or fear.

Such regimes promote false news in a systematic campaign of disinformation, even as they go after independent voices.

America is still a fairly open society in which assertions can be independently verified and a thriving Internet community can tear apart false allegations. Even in the United States, though, opinion is being penalized, and false news is being disseminated which disorients the public.

Early on in the Bush administration, the press experienced unusually quick, tough pushback: The White House told reporters critical of the administration that they could be cut out of the information loop. This is aggressive, but still fair game as part of democracy's playbook.

Then the pushback escalated to personal smears. When antiterror czar Richard Clarke wrote *Against All Enemies*, the White House tried to discredit him by sending into the news stream negative personal information. Again, this approach, though unattractive, is still part of democratic debate. Personal smears in the press go back to Revolutionary America.

But starting in 2003, people who published or broadcast information damaging to the administration began to lose their jobs. Diplomat Joseph Wilson's wife, CIA operative Valerie Plame, was famously "outed" by Deputy Secretary of State Richard Armitage and possibly by Lewis "Scooter" Libby, Cheney's chief of staff, in retaliation against her husband's op-ed in *The New York Times* arguing that the "weapons of mass destruction" rationale for the war in Iraq was based on false information.[1]

In 2004, Dan Rather, then-*CBS News* anchor, ran a segment on the show on documents that purported to detail George Bush's failure to show up for his duties during the Vietnam War as a member of the Texas Air National Guard. When it became clear that the documents were fake, a powerful Republican PR group—Creative Response Concepts, the same group that led the Swift Boat Veterans for Truth to attack John Kerry's campaign in 2004—led an aggressive right-wing media and blogger push against Rather. Rather was forced into early retirement.[2]

Then the Bush administration began to exert job pressure on employees of PBS and NPR.

Public Radio and Television

The Public Broadcasting System was reconfigured in 2004 after the Bush administration installed a supporter, Kenneth Tomlinson, as chair of the Corporation for Public Broadcasting. Tomlinson hired a firm to tabulate a list accounting for the political leanings of different pundits involved with PBS, in order to purge the network of its "liberal" bias.[3] (Goebbels had done the same to state radio employees in 1933). Press reports played this out, once more, as absurd overreaching, and Tomlinson resigned in 2005. However, the net effect of the tally's being now public was to let the chattering classes know that their political tendencies may be tracked by the state.

The next year, in July of 2006, Melanie Martinez, a presenter for a PBS children's show, *The Good Night Show*, was discovered to have, years earlier, acted in a video spoof of abstinence education programs.

PBS executives fired her. They did not claim that she had lied on her resume or in any way failed to do her job. They just noted that the video made her "inappropriate" for the role. There is hardly an employee of PBS or NPR who has not engaged in political speech at one time. PBS's own ombudsman, Michael Getler, wrote that Ms. Martinez's firing had "too much of a whiff of after-the-fact loyalty oaths and purity checks on performers who do lots of different things."[4]

This is just a kids' TV show. But recall that this tactic tends to begin inoffensively, but set a precedent. PBS also does news coverage and debates. Many viewers have begun to notice a more reserved tone on PBS.

In a climate in which they face orchestrated smear campaigns, reporters will still report critical stories. But in a climate in which they can lose their jobs—as Bill Maher and Dan Rather did—many will tread more carefully.

Threaten the Press with Prison at Home and with Violence Abroad

No one hurts reporters in the United States in 2007. But reporters are getting hurt under U.S. oversight in Iraq in circumstances that journalists' rights organizations have called suspicious.

In 2003, respected BBC correspondent Kate Adie told Irish Radio in an interview that the Pentagon had threatened to fire on independent reporters' locations from the air—to "target down"—if they detected the electronic signals that indicated that the reporters were transmitting stories. Adie said that when a senior Pentagon officer was asked about the possibility that reporters might be killed, he replied, "Who cares . . . they've been warned." Adie also said that the U.S. military was demanding that independent reporters reveal their political positions on the war.[5]

By the beginning of April 2003, administration figures such as Defense Secretary Donald Rumsfeld were attacking the coverage of the war in Iraq by unembedded journalists. They singled out *Al-Jazeera* in particular. April became a bloody month for unembedded journalists in Iraq.

The organization Reporters Without Borders noted that on April 8, 2003, "three journalists were killed by the U.S. army in a single day." Al-Jazeera cameraman and bureau chief, Tarek Ayoub, 35, died when a U.S. missile hit the offices of Al-Jazeera. Reporters' rights organizations claimed that U.S. forces appeared to target the Palestine Hotel in Baghdad. Reuters cameraman Taras Protsyuk, 35, died as well, as did a 27-year-old Spanish cameraman. "The places targeted were all known to be used by journalists but the U.S. army investigation brazenly cleared all those involved," protested the journalists' organization.

The organization claims that, contrary to the U.S. military's assertion that the United States fired at the Palestine Hotel in self-defense, in fact the firing was unprovoked. "We are appalled at what happened because it was known that both places contained journalists," said the group's secretary-general Robert Menard. He notes that film shot by a French TV station shows that the area was quiet, "and that the US tank crew took their time, waiting for a couple of minutes and adjusting its gun before opening fire. This evidence does not match the US version of an attack in self-defense and we can only conclude that the US army deliberately and without warning targeted journalists. . . . Very many non-embedded journalists have complained of . . . being held and interrogated for several hours. One group of non-embedded journalists was held in secret for two days and roughed up by the US military police," Menard said.[6]

Robert Fisk, the well-known correspondent for *The Independent*, had been at Al-Jazeera's offices in Baghdad on April 4. He had told Ayoub that Ayoub's office would make an easy target if the United States wanted to take it out. "Don't worry, Robert," Ayoub had said, reassuring Fisk that the Al-Jazeera team knew it was safe—after all, it had alerted U.S. forces of its exact position a few days before.[7]

Even Al-Jazeera believes that America would keep reporters safe.

A year later journalists were still at risk. According to Amy Goodman's interview with Al-Jazeera reporter Ahmed Mansur on *Democracy Now!*, and also according to Jeremy Scahill in *The Nation,* senior military spokesman Mark Kimmitt had announced that stations such as Al-Jazeera that were filming American soldiers killing women and children in Fallujah were not legitimate news sources but "propaganda."[8] The U.K. *Daily Mirror* reported that at about the same time, Bush had told Prime Minister Tony Blair that he wanted to bomb Al-Jazeera.[9] On April 15, 2004, Donald Rumsfeld declared that Al-Jazeera's coverage of the siege of Fallujah was "vicious, inaccurate and inexcusable. It's disgraceful what the station is doing."[10]

An Al-Jazeera cameraman has been held by the U.S. for almost six years. Kristof describes what happened to 37-year-old college-educated, English-speaking Al-Jazeera cameraman, Sami al-Hajj. Al-Hajj was detained by the United States while covering the war in Afghanistan. In the American military prison in Bagram, he was "repeatedly beaten, kicked, starved, left out in the freezing cold and subjected to anal cavity searches in public." Six months later he was flown to Guantánamo and also brutally beaten. His interrogators claimed he had obtained video footage of Osama bin Laden, but that claim fell apart when it seemed that they had confused al-Hajj with someone with a similar name. They made many other accusations but scarcely followed up on them in interrogations, preferring to try to get dirt on Al-Jazeera.

According to his lawyer, the interrogators told Mr. Hajj that he would be freed immediately if he agree to spy on his employer.

When al-Hajj asked what would happen if he did not do so, "You would not do that," Mr. Hajj quoted his interrogator as saying, "because it would endanger your child."[11]

It is not just journalists from "alien" news outlets such as Al-Jazeera who face risks from U.S. forces in Iraq: CBS and AP staff have also been singled out.

Larry Doyle, the CBS News bureau chief in Baghdad, received an e-mail at 10 p.m. on March 21, 2006, telling him that his cameraman, Abdul Ameer Younis Hussein, would face a trial in less than twelve hours. Mr. Hussein's lawyers were given no notice of the trial at all. Mr. Hussein had been wounded by the U.S. military and taken into custody.[12] (Reporters Without Borders had demanded an investigation of the incident: "Once again the US forces have targeted a journalist just doing his job."[13])

Doyle said that CBS was "stymied" in trying to find out what evidence there might be against his staffer. Hussein was held for a year at Abu Ghraib. "All we are seeking is due process for Mr. Hussein," said CBS spokeswoman Sandy Genelius.[14] The little information his colleagues could uncover about his arrest indicated that a U.S. task force had claimed that Hussein "appeared to be instigating a crowd" in Mosul, but those charges against the man were not made public. For a more than two years, no one at CBS was able to find out the charges or evidence against him. He faced life in prison if convicted. Hussein was eventually cleared of all charges by the Iraqi attorney general.[15]

AP couldn't keep its employees safe either: The U.S. military in Iraq imprisoned Pulitzer Prize–winning AP photographer, Bilal Hussein (no relation to the CBS cameraman), in April 2006, claiming that he was a security threat. Bilal Hussein's images of women and children suffering in the war are famous. But U.S. authorities have never filed charges or allowed a public hearing: "We want the rule of law to prevail," said Tom Curley, AP president and CEO. "He either needs to be charged or released."

But Major General Jack Gardner e-mailed AP's international

editor that "[Bilal Hussein] has close relationships with persons known to be responsible for kidnappings, smuggling, improvised explosive device attacks and other attacks on coalition forces."[16] This jeopardizes all of us who are reporters: any decent reporter will eventually have to develop "relationships"—even "close relationships"—with sources who are very bad people, in order to do their jobs. Many Pulitzer Prizes have been won because a story started with a journalist closely befriending a very nasty person.

If you have not heard much about these two cases, it may be because CBS and AP management, understandably, do not want to jeopardize their imprisoned staff further.

But imagine what it means today to be the head of CBS News or AP—and know that you can't get one of your reporters a fair trial, let alone get him or her out of jail. Yes, all this happened in a country far away. But do these arrests have no ripple effect in our own nation? Does that act of state terror not send a message to the community of journalists here at home—even if just in the form of informal gossip? And if one were a reporter for such an organization, would one not be hesitant—if only unconsciously—to write something that might enrage the administration and jeopardize one's colleague further?

In a closing society, reporters start to get hurt more directly.

Right now, Russia claims some of the trappings of a democracy. But in 2006, famed reporter Anna Politkovskaya, who reported on truths that the government wanted to suppress about Chechnya, was shot to death in her apartment building.[17] In January of 2007, newspaper editor Hrant Dink, who published truths the government did not want exposed about the massacre of Armenians in that country, was shot and killed in Turkey.[18] The people who committed both murders will probably get away with them. That is what can happen to reporters and editors in countries that aren't truly free.

Though no one threatens reporters physically in the United States, they are facing new threats of other kinds. It is standard practice for dictators to start to recategorize the gathering of news as "a threat to national security." This prepares the way for further targeting: On a U.S. Army Website in 2007, the media is listed as another threat, alongside "al-Qaeda," "warloards," and "drug cartels."[19] The *Columbia Journalism Review* warned that this sends "the unambiguous message to soldiers and DoD employees that reporters are to be treated as enemies."[20]

Reporters are facing escalating numbers of investigations and subpoenas in the United States. In August 2006, a New York appeals court ruled that the prosecutor could seize Judith Miller and reporter Philip Shenon's phone records from a story they were reporting on an Islamic charity.[21] Time Inc.'s editors warned their reporters that "Most electronic records, including e-mail, can be subpoenaed and retrieved in litigation."[22] David Barstow, a reporter at *The New York Times*, told *The Observer* that his newspaper had begun legal seminars to help reporters avoid what executive editor Bill Keller called "the persistent legal perils that confront us." "With this crazy environment, with subpoenas and so on, there is this feeling that you have to act like a drug dealer or a Mafioso . . . [A subpoena is] just no longer an abstract threat," said Barstow. A columnist in *The Observer* wrote that some of the advice given to reporters in these seminars had "the sound of advice for reporting behind the Iron Curtain before the fall—recalling A.M. Rosenthal burning his notes as a reporter in Communist Poland."[23]

You might not just be subpoenaed as a reporter: You might face charges yourself. In August 2006, the Department of Homeland Security accused Greg Palast, author of the bestselling critique of the administration, *Armed Madhouse*, and TV producer Matt Pascarella of "unauthorized filming of a 'critical national security structure.'" Palast and Pascarella were in Louisiana, filming evacuees who had been made homeless by Hurricane Katrina. They filmed an ExxonMobil refinery behind the encampment, to give a sense of how unhealthful the setting was for children and the elderly.

Shortly thereafter, Palast got a call from Detective Frank

Pananepinto: Palast was facing charges for the filming. Palast's tone on his blog is upbeat: "Matt and I look pretty good in orange." But it is also anxious: "First, this ain't no foolin' around: Matt and I are facing these nutty charges."[24]

This is what it sounds like when the ground starts to shift from a democracy to something less. There are variations in tone: Is this a joke? Or am I really in trouble?

One such story is kind of funny—if it ends there. But thirty such stories make a "tipping point." In the histories of the closing down of open societies, it doesn't take many such events for things to change entirely.

Control of the Press in the Past

"As long as I have a pen in my hand and a revolver in my pocket, I fear no man," wrote Mussolini, who had been a newspaper editor.[25] Each fascist leader we have been looking at has sought aggressively to control the press and been successful at securing that control in short order.

By 1923, Fascist prefects were permitted by the leadership in Rome to take possession of newspapers and demand fines from the publishers if the newspapers published something that could "damage national credit at home or abroad," alarm and dismay public opinion and so disturb "order." The edict that provided for this was ambiguously worded—as so many Fascist edicts are—in order to ensure that the press would curtail its own freedom. Mussolini created a registry system to make sure the Italian press toed the line: All reporters had to register as Fascist by 1928. This method would be imitated precisely by Goebbels. Mussolini justified this control over the press in the name of patriotism: "Discipline" over the news, it was claimed, writes Bosworth, "served in the interests of the nation."[26]

Mussolini also understood that it was crucial for him to gain control of public radio—which of course, at the time, was popular culture. By 1925 Mussolini had created an investigative commission, the EIAR, to tighten government control of public radio. A substantial Fascist film industry was developed after 1933.[27]

In closing or closed societies, reporters are arrested for revealing "state secrets" or "classified information": in 1931, for instance, the influential left-wing editor Carl Ossietzky was sentenced to 18 months in prison for publishing documents that showed that the German army was engaged in combat that violated the Treaty of Versailles; he would be arrested, released, rearrested, and tortured throughout the Nazi era and, despite an international outcry and a Nobel Prize, he would die from the abuse he suffered.[28]

During the 1933 purges in Germany, Goebbels fired 13 percent of the state radio's employees in six months. The radio staff that were fired were not only Jews but also Liberals, Social Democrats, and others not in harmony with the new regime. Radio managers and reporters who were seen as being friendly to the prior liberal broadcasting regime were arrested on corruption charges and taken to Oranienberg concentration camp, where they were condemned in a huge show trial the following year.[29]

In Communist China after the prodemocracy protests of 1989, reporters were targeted as well. "The authorities harassed us, denounced us and almost expelled us from the country," wrote Kristof and WuDunn, "In at least eighteen cases since . . . 1978 Chinese have gone to prison or labor camp for terms of up to life imprisonment because they helped foreign correspondents."[30]

False News and Faked Documents

"The great masses of the people will more easily fall victims of a big lie than a small one," Hitler wrote in *Mein Kampf*. Fascists rely on "perception management"—what the intelligence community calls "info ops"—because their tactics won't stand scrutiny by a free press. So in a fascist shift, as real reporters are being frozen out, smeared, or faced with unemployment, there is an increasing use of spectacle in conveying "message"—and the spectacle is accompanied by the production of fake news and false documents.

The messaging, combined with the spectacle, can be stunning in a fascist ascendancy. Fascist messaging has advantages that democratic communications and advocacy, even of the highest sophistication, just can't demonstrate: You can use a monolithic, harmonized voice and vision, unimpeded by dissent, rather than trying to break though a clash of pluralistic arguments. This power of epic messaging in combination with the power of spectacle is a well-known aspect of the seduction of fascism.

Goebbels coordinated the Nazi message with the monumental sets, blazing klieg lighting, and heroic backdrops that architect Albert Speer designed. The sets conveyed might and permanence—the thousand-year Reich that it would be hopeless to contest. Hitler, who had been trained as a visual artist, also understood the emotional power of spectacle: He commissioned a young filmmaker named Leni Riefenstahl to create *Triumph of the Will*, a classic propaganda film. Hitler admired her Nordic risk-taking persona and wanted her to create that magic for him. Riefenstahl's film was shown again and again to German movie audiences and saturated their consciousnesses, creating a sense of invincibility around Hitler and the Nazis.

Riefenstahl had begun her career as a daredevil action film actress. In *SOS Iceberg*, she flies a small plane—by herself—and lands it dramatically. She also crafted a scene in an early film of her own that shows a young Nazi war hero greeted by admirers as he opens the door of his small plane.

Triumph of the Will repeats this motif: Hitler's plane descends through the clouds and lands. Uniformed paramilitary personnel and civilians gather around the plane's door to welcome him. Hitler emerges to review his troops, who are dressed identically and massed in orderly rows. Hitler is wearing his own uniform, a black leather belt and a black leather bandolier across his chest. His tan jodhpurs are tucked into black leather boots and he carries a military hat in his left hand. Some sceenes later, Hitler greets and addresses the vast, orderly mass of troops in an epic scene of the troops hailing their leader. Huge vertical banners are visible throughout the crowd. Backing the parade ground is Speer's enormous stylized eagle with its wings outspread, in the center of which is a circle containing the intersecting lines of a swastika. In another film of the Nuremberg Rally speeches, Hitler says, "I ask . . . for your support for the accomplishment of this mission . . . ours is a great mission."

In the "Mission Accomplished" photo opportunity, Bush descends over water, in a small plane that he is copiloting. He lands on an aircraft carrier, where he emerges to review and address the gathered troops. Uniformed military personnel clamor to open his plane's door and welcome him.

Bush is dressed in a green flight suit with many leather straps and with a great deal of hardware across the chest. He is wearing black leather boots and holds his helmet in his left hand. A massive horizontal banner reading "Mission Accomplished" stretches behind him. The troops are standing in a vast expanse of orderly rows. Their cheering lasts for long minutes.

The USS *Lincoln* event was stage-managed by a team of TV production experts: Scott Sforza, a former ABC producer; Bob DeServi, a former NBC cameraman and lighting expert; and Greg Jenkins, formerly a Fox News producer. According to Elisabeth Bumiller, the team orchestrated every aspect of the visuals of the event, "even down to the members of the Lincoln crew arrayed in coordinated shirt colors over Mr. Bush's right shoulder." The President's remarks were delivered during what film and TV producers call "magic hour light," which cast a golden glow on Mr. Bush."[31]

Propaganda is part of both fascist and democratic advocacy: American political ads, for instance, are a form of propaganda. But, while exaggeration and "spin" are part of democracy's playbook, flat-out lies and false documents are not.

Dictatorships specialize in faking news and falsifying documents. Hitler wrote that "all effective propaganda must be limited to a very few points and must harp on these in slogans until the last member of the public understands what you want him to understand . . ." He argued that good propaganda speaks to feelings and not reason, and that "it should never admit a glimmer of doubt in its own claims, or concede the tiniest element of right in the claims of the other side," according to Evans.[32]

To back up its disinformation campaigns, such regimes often rely on false documents. These counterfeit documents often assert that there is a threat to the home population. As Orwell satirized this tactic in *Animal Farm*, "[Snowball] was Jones's secret agent all the time. It has all been proved by documents which he left behind him and which we have only just discovered."[33]

On May 10, 1940, Colonel Joachim von Ribbentrop explained at a press conference that the Reich had found it necessary to send its troops to invade the Low Countries in order "to safeguard the neutrality of Belgium and Holland." William Shirer called this assertion "nonsensical hypocrisy" and noted with disgust that it was "backed up" by a faked document that purported to show that those countries were about to invade the Ruhr.[34] Nazi propagandists also claimed—falsely—that three million ethnic [Sudeten] Germans in Czechoslovakia were being persecuted and abused.[35]

After Pinochet's coup, TV and magazines showed the images of the arms caches that the coup leaders claimed to have found in the homes of the leaders of the opposition party. (A series of images from Iraq have shown such arms caches too, the weapons lined up in neat stacks). The Chilean coup leaders also published a "white book" on "Plan Z"—the elaborate conspiracy that they claimed had been set in motion to kill a group of Chile's leaders simultaneously. Some Chileans believed that "Plan Z" was real; others believed that the charges were trumped up to provide an excuse to take over the country.[36] But it didn't really matter.

After a certain point in a fascist shift, it doesn't matter whether most people believe the faked news or not—eventually they simply don't have access to enough good information to assess what is real and what is not. In accounts of the Chinese prodemocracy uprising in 1989, you can hear well-intentioned Chinese citizens struggling with this: The Voice of America radio station was reporting on the uprising accurately, describing the protesters as idealistic students—but the Politburo was accusing the VOA of spreading unpatriotic lies. Chinese state TV, print, and radio called the protesters counterrevolutionary "criminals" and "ruffians." Citizens, frightened by this, were writing letters to their newspapers haplessly explaining that they had diligently compared the VOA reports and the Politburo reports—and they found the Politburo reports to be more accurate.

I find those citizens' struggles to sift truth from lies to be so moving. At that point, the state had made truth fungible.

History shows us some reasons why the administration may be so intent on sending lies into the press stream and accusing those who tell the truth of lying.

Perhaps the barrage of lies serves a more substantial purpose than simply advancing a certain position. Sending a current of lies into the information stream is part of classic psychological operations to generate a larger shift—a new reality in which the truth *can no longer be ascertained and no longer counts.*

In this reality citizens no longer feel empowered or able to establish the truth on either side—and therefore give up their agency. At this point people can be manipulated into supporting almost any state action. For how can citizens know what is right? Truth itself has been cheapened, made subjective and internal, not absolute and external.

Frank Rich, Sidney Blumenthal, Amy Goodman, and Joe Conason have all impressively documented the outright lies of the

White House. In *The Greatest Story Ever Sold: The Decline and Fall of Truth*, Rich singles out the fake "yellowcake in Niger" and "mobile biological and chemical weapons labs" stories, both of which led us into war. According to polls, Rich noted, 51 percent of Americans in 2003 believed that Iraqis were personally involved in 9/11. Not only were the "yellowcake" documents cited in the State of the Union speech fake, but Rich shows that the White House then lied about those lies. He demonstrates that the administration lied about the claim that Mohammed Atta met with a senior Iraqi official in Prague—and then lied about *that* lie.[37] Reports in 2005 noted that the Department of Education created faked independent TV features and sent them to local stations (Goebbels sent out progovernment newsreels and gramophone records through the mail to be shown around the country, an innovation at the time). And conservative columnist Armstrong Williams earned $241,000 from the Department of Education to promote the No Child Left Behind program.[38]

Critics have exposed the role of The Lincoln Group, a Washington-based PR firm, which secured a lucrative contract from the Bush administration to place false news supportive of the United States in Iraqi media. In September 2006, *The New York Times* reported that the Bush administration had been paying reporters for *The Miami Herald* for certain kinds of positive coverage.[39]

Why does this matter so much? Why does a government's promotion of lying help facilitate a fascist shift? What does the truth have to do with democracy?

Democracy depends on a social agreement that is so obvious to us that it usually goes unspoken: There *is* such thing as truth. In an open society, we know facts may be hedged and spun in the back-and-forth of debate, but truth is the ground *from which* the hedging or spinning begin. Democracy depends upon accountability; accountability requires us to be able to tell truth from lies; and to be able to tell truth from lies, we all first must agree that truth matters.

If the ground of democracy is truth, the ground of dictatorship is assertion. In a dictatorship, reality belongs to whoever has the greatest power to assert.

Critics such as Goodman, Rich, and Conason are engaged in a valuable public service by exposing the government's lies. But they are still participating in the game of democracy: someone lies, you expose the lie—like a tennis tournament in which there is a net and a score and impartial referees.

In democracy, lying is at most a sneaky tactic in the game. But in a fascist system, lies are the game board itself. Why should Soviet leaders have bothered to have party members who had been purged airbrushed out of official photographs? Not just to diminish their memory—but to assert to citizens that the state held power over memory itself. Why, in *Animal Farm*, do the pigs, the ruling caste, erase elements of their mission statement, and then deny to the other animals that they have done so? Not simply to advance a specific outcome, but also to make the other animals lose their ability to trust in their own judgment.

Orwell wrote of "a nightmare world in which the Leader, or some ruling clique, controls not only the future *but the past.*"[40]

Tom Kean, the cochair of the 9/11 commission, OK'd an ABC miniseries, to be broadcast without commercials on the five-year anniversary of 9/11, that portrayed scenes of former Clinton White House staff that were fictional. The made-up scenes showed, for instance, former national security advisor Sandy Berger hanging up on a CIA official at a crucial moment in a military action and former Secretary of State Madeleine Albright allowing Osama bin Laden to slip away from capture. Albright told Disney, ABC's owner, that the miniseries "depicted scenes that never happened, events that never took place, decisions that were never made and conversations that never occurred."[41]

Kean was unapologetic. According to the *New York Post*, "he was all right with the made-up scene—even though the video is being peddled to high schools as a teaching aid."[42]

Remember the voices of Chinese citizens struggling to make sense of their own recent history—and getting it heartbreakingly wrong. How can they know otherwise?

Now listen to Tom Kean introduce a new epistemology into American discourse: An ordinary lie distorts or hides the truth; the fascist lie is the assertion that truth is not a marker anymore. "I don't think the facts are clear whether Sandy Berger, if the CIA [hung up] or if the line went dead," Kean said. "But they [the producers] chose to portray it this way. My memory is that it could have happened any number of ways."[43]

"It could have happened any number of ways."

When part of *Animal Farm*'s mission statement is erased,

> All the animals remembered passing such resolutions: or at least they thought that they remembered it. . . . Squealer . . . assured them that the resolution against engaging in trade and using money had never been passed, or even suggested. It was pure imagination, probably traceable in the beginning to lies circulated by Snowball. A few animals still felt faintly doubtful, but Squealer asked them shrewdly, "Are you certain this is not something you have dreamed, comrades? Have you any record of such a resolution? Is it written down anywhere?"[44]

"A little girl Rambo." Pat Tillman's heroic death. John Kerry's Purple Heart. The Iraq War death toll.

Are you certain this is all not something you have dreamed, my fellow Americans?

Once you accomplish this flooding of the plain of discourse with lies, you are much closer to closing down an open society. If citizens can't be sure you are telling the truth or not, you can manipulate people into supporting almost anything the state wants to undertake; and it is also much more difficult for citizens to advocate or mobilize on their own behalf: How can they be sure what is right and what is wrong?

At a time such as this, it is up to U.S. citizens who are not part of the formal media world to publish online, research aggressively, check facts assiduously, expose abuses, file Freedom of Information Act requests, publish 'zines, write op-eds, and take ownership of producing as much of the news and information stream as they can. Above all, you need to push through the laws proposed by the American Freedom Agenda and the American Freedom Campaign, so that journalists will be shielded from threats and prosecution.

Blogging has to lead the way, because this is the access point for citizen journalism. But bloggers must take their impact far more seriously, becoming warriors for truth and accountability: Citizens have to start to produce reliable *samizdat.* Opinion is important, but opinion alone is totally inadequate when the ground of truth itself is under assault. Bloggers must become rigorous and fearless documentarians and reporters—not just to critique the news, but also to generate the news. Citizens in every venue must now apply to their work the accuracy and accountability that news editors have traditionally expected of their writers and researchers. The locus of the power of truth must be identified not in major news outlets but in you. You—not "they"—must take responsibility for educating your fellow citizens.

It was librarians, schoolteachers, booksellers, and small publishers who helped to push back dictators in countries where speech was under attack. Journalists are in the line of fire now; but history shows that these producers and distributors of free speech are next in line.

In the Revolutionary era, farmers, artisans, and small shopkeepers read and wrote pamphlets, distributed broadsheets, gave speeches at town assemblies, and ripped essays from the presses in order to debate with one another the points they made. They didn't subcontract out the patriot's task of speaking up to a professional pundit class. They saw their own voices as being vitally necessary to the crafting of the Constitution and, even more important, to the life of the new nation.

We have to abandon the passive role we have accepted as mere consumers of media; we must see ourselves in a new light—or rather, see ourselves once again in a Revolutionary light—as citizen leaders with responsibilities to speak the truth.

— CHAPTER TEN —

CAST CRITICISM *as* "ESPIONAGE" *and* DISSENT *as* "TREASON"

Treason against the United States, shall consist only in levying War against them, or in adhering to their Enemies, giving them Aid and Comfort.

ARTICLE 3, U.S. CONSTITUTION

The Constitution defines *treason* as actually "levying war" against America or giving "aid and comfort" to its enemies. The Founders intentionally made it difficult to throw around the term *traitor*, which had so often been used to intimidate the Revolutionary generation.

But in every fascist shift, more and more kinds of speech and protest become cast as "treason," "terrorism," "subversion," "espionage" or "sabotage." (A charge of "slander" tends to prepare the ground first: In Stalin's Russia, criticism of the state was first defined as "slander" and then redefined as "treason." Ann Coulter's book *Slander* was published one year in advance of her book, *Treason.*)

The Bush team is trying to move "treason" from its narrow Constitutional definition to a looser definition. The smear of treason has a long, ugly—and unfortunately time-tested—history of use by mid-twentieth-century dictators, as do the accusations of sabotage and espionage. The Bush administration has started to use the notion of treason in its Stalinist sense: as a weapon designed to harass critics and to frighten opposition leaders.

In a fascist shift, as I've noted, leaders introduce and then seek to establish new categories of offenses that criminalize citizens' ideas, actions, or speech. This is an important turning point. The next step is that new laws or new interpretations of existing laws attach new criminal penalties for these acts of "treason." As this verbal "third rail" becomes established, certain subjects become too charged to address, or begin to be avoided altogether, because addressing them carries possible criminal penalties. The *Heimtuckegesetz* law of 1934 in Germany criminalized political libel and slander. Though penalties were not usually severe under this law, the prosecutions were many: more than 100,000.[1] People were being sent to prison for telling jokes. Klemperer notes about the jokes of the day that "Conversations in heaven are popular. The best one: Hitler to Moses: 'But you can tell me in confidence, Herr Moses. Is it not true that you set the bush on fire yourself?'" The man who told this joke was sentenced to ten months in prison.[2] In cold-war Czechoslovakia, if you read banned printed material—*samizdat*—you were *not* committing a crime, but if you handed the material to a friend, you *had* committed a crime.

Right-wing pundit Coulter's 2003 bestseller *Treason* repackaged the "speech-as-treason" concept for post–World War II U.S. popular culture. Coulter's book introduced "treason" as a legitimate term to characterize the opinions of artists, entertainers, and press critical of the Bush administration: "While the form of treachery varies slightly from case to case, liberals always manage to take the position that most undermines American security."[3] In 2003, this approach was a rhetorical feint with no real consequences. However, four years on, with the invocation of the Espionage Act, a piece of rhetoric becomes something much more serious. Coulter re-introduces the idea that in wartime America, speech, so long as it is identified as "treason," can be criminally prosecuted.

> Fortunately for Hollywood liberals and former Democratic presidents, the country discontinued prosecuting treason long ago. . . . World War II–era traitors were prosecuted and sentenced to long prison terms for radio broadcasts heard

> by no one within America. . . . Axis Sally was sentenced to twelve years in prison. Tokyo Rose got six years in prison. Hanoi Jane makes aerobics videos.
>
> During the Vietnam War, Fonda gave wild, inflammatory anti-American speeches from Hanoi. . . . At the time, serious thought was given to prosecuting her, but the ruling class was equivocal about treason. The refusal to prosecute Fonda was just one more indication that we weren't fighting that war to win. . . .[4]

The "treason" rollout continued: on June 23, 2006, when *The New York Times* published the SWIFT banking story, the rhetoric of treason was put to use in a new way: Though *New York Times* executive editor Bill Keller pointed out that the administration itself had boasted of the program, a right-wing push to criminalize what Keller had done ensued.

President Bush personally called the publication of the story "disgraceful." A week later, a Republican Congressman called for an investigation and a special prosecutor. Right-wing blogs exploded with the themes of "treason" and "crime." Right-wing pundits began to call in unison for Bush to invoke the 1917 Espionage Act against the publisher and editors of *The New York Times.*[5]

In San Francisco, KSFO radio host Melanie Morgan "called for *New York Times* editor Bill Keller's potential execution if both charged and found guilty of treason." She said:

> I made it clear with my very first words that I saw this as a case of treason. Yes, for those of you in the "cut and run" crowd, I said TREASON.
>
> [Chris] Matthews was shocked. He seemed to think he misunderstood me. I couldn't have really meant that, could I? Long prison sentences for reporters because they repeatedly leaked classified information on America's efforts to combat terrorism?

> Absolutely.
>
> . . . *New York Times* editor Bill Keller and his accomplices should face prosecution by the government of the United States for willfully and repeatedly undermining the war effort against terrorism by repeatedly violating the law and reporting on classified anti-terrorism programs.[6]

(Nikolai Bukharin, the editor-in-chief of *Izvestia,* who had been a critic of Stalin, was accused of "espionage" and "treason" in the Moscow show trials, found guilty—and actually executed.[7])

The blogosphere also invoked the 1917 Espionage Act. *Weekly Standard* editor William Kristol demanded that the Justice Department prosecute the *Times* under the Espionage Act.[8] National Review Online contributing editor Deroy Murdock wrote:

> Strict punishment for the *Times*'s crimes (and it has behaved criminally) is in order. . . . So, what is to be done with this irresponsible rag? . . . Congress in 1950 passed something called the "Comint statute". . . . the resulting law, U.S. Criminal Code Title 18, Section 798, reads:
>
> "Whoever knowingly and willfully communicates, furnishes, transmits, or otherwise makes available to an unauthorized person, or *publishes*, or uses in any manner prejudicial to the safety or interest of the United States or for the benefit of any foreign government to the detriment of the United States any *classified information . . . concerning the communication intelligence activities of the United States* . . . shall be fined not more than $10,000 or imprisoned not more than ten years, or both."

Murdock concluded: "Under this law, and perhaps also the 1917 Espionage Act, the *Times* deserves to be indicted immediately for its NSA and Swift stories."[9]

During the Swift banking story controversy, conservative pundits' calls for the prosecution of the *Times* were still rhetorical—still a play, if a rough one, in an open society's game.

But the Justice Department was actually using the Espionage Act, and not rhetorically any more: In 2005, it prosecuted two former lobbyists for the American Israel Public Affairs Committee, Steve Rosen and Keith Weissman, for having accepted a leak from a government employee.[10] The 1917 Espionage Act makes it illegal for an unauthorized person to have "unlawful possession" of "information relating to the national defense." This revived use of the law could potentially criminalize conversations in many serious newsrooms—not to mention even conversation at many frivolous Washington dinner parties.

And if the Justice Department only goes after reporters who disclose classified information—as did the reporters who exposed the Pentagon Papers and My Lai—you still have a minefield: This administration classifies and declassifies material continually. If this new benchmark prevails, American reporters can be charged, convicted, and sent to prison for tripping over any number of newly electrified tripwires: if you run a photograph of Vice President Cheney's house that inadvertently reveals where security staff are posted; if you publish an expose of interrogation conditions at Abu Ghraib, as Seymour Hersh did. GIs who write books about their Iraq experiences and inadvertently reveal troop movements, diplomats who write op-eds like Joseph Wilson's exposé of the yellowcake claim, which was based on classified documents—all these Americans could be prosecuted.

Historically the shift from rhetoric to reality happens quickly. Based on the historical blueprint, one can guess that it wouldn't take long not only for "espionage" but for "treason" too, to move from inflammatory accusations to criminal charges.

Three years after Ann Coulter's book asked us to imagine this possibility, on October 12, 2006, the Justice Department charged the first American in more than half a century with treason. Adam

Gadahn, a young Southern Californian who is accused of helping al-Qaeda create videotapes urging violence against the United States, was charged in a sealed indictment in a California federal court. As in Padilla's case, officials do not claim to have evidence that Mr. Gadahn has taken part in planning terrorist attacks against the United States. His words are his crime. Paul McNulty, the Deputy Attorney General, said that Gadahn provided the enemy with "aid and comfort" by acting as a propagandist for Al Qaeda.[11] Making such propaganda is wrong, but a frightening precedent has been set. For anyone, even those who are not even on a battlefield or in a war zone, a charge of treason carries a possible death sentence.

If you don't know anything about the 1917 Espionage Act, it sounds kind of salutary. In 1917, the nation was at war; of course we need to root out spies during wartime. But its history is sinister.

In the nineteen-teens, a wave of left-wing activism swept the nation. Many of the activists working for better conditions and higher wages were also against the nation's entry into the war.

So as the country prepared for war, President Woodrow Wilson's communications machine issued a wave of propaganda to whip up war fervor. Congress quickly passed the 1917 Espionage and Trading with the Enemy Act, which criminalized antiwar remarks. Hundreds of American citizens were prosecuted for objecting to military recruitment or for speaking or writing things that could remotely be interpreted as dissent from the government's line. Citizens' meetings were raided by government spies and there were sweeping arrests without warrants. It was against the law under the 1917 Espionage Act to mail an antiwar opinion or even to advocate for a referendum on whether or not the United States should enter the war. Officials of the post office leaked files on antiwar "traitors" to newspapers.

Sentences were severe: A Kansas City man got ten years in prison for having written a letter to a newspaper. A mother of four criticized the war and got five years in jail. Eugene Debs, the Socialist candidate, tried to challenge the Act in 1918, invoking the

First Amendment. Debs was found guilty and was sentenced to ten years.[12]

The Palmer Raids were the culmination of these events. Attorney General A. Mitchell Palmer used the 1917 Espionage Act and the 1918 Sedition Act to gather information on 260,000 citizens; the raids arrested 10,000 citizens as well as immigrants in 1919. The mass arrests were warrantless and the authorities created fake documents to deport whom they could. Teachers, librarians, and working men and women were jailed. Scores in Connecticut alone were "beaten, starved, suffocated, tortured and threatened with death in futile efforts to extract confessions." But in spite of all these arrests and imprisonments, evidence to support Palmer's accusations of a revolutionary network never surfaced.[13]

The pendulum swung back: a group of patriotic lawyers, led by future Supreme Court justice Felix Frankfurter, issued a report calling the raids and arrests "utterly illegal." Palmer's power waned. Nonetheless, the fear remained. After the Palmer raids, many Americans were scared to subscribe to certain journals; teachers policed what they said in the classroom; editors weighed their words. Dissent was muted for a decade. People turned their energies to safer matters than activism: flappers, talkies, and bathtub gin.[14]

"Sabotage" is another of these code words: Stalin's arrests of 1937 frequently accused people of sabotage. On February 15, 2007, Republican Congressman Don Young said: "Congressmen who willfully take actions during wartime that damage morale and undermine the military are *saboteurs*, and should be arrested, exiled or *hanged*" [*italics mine*].[15] (In the U.S., executions take place by lethal injection; death by hanging was a 20th century dictator's method of execution.)

Often the laws that criminalize dissent in a fascist shift are enacted quietly. In November of 2006, the Senate passed The Animal

Enterprise Terrorism Act—which allows federal prosecutors to "enhance" prison terms for convicted activists. When I first saw this, I thought that it was likely that soon an American environmentalist or animal rights activist would be prosecuted severely under "terrorism enhancement" guidelines aimed at crimes against animal processing facilities. Indeed, those trials began seven months later. The "terrorists" being sentenced for attacks on commercial processing facilities now looked like the boys and girls next door.

New terms join *treason* and *espionage* to criminalize citizens themselves, who can suddenly become "enemies of the people," "disturbers of the peace," "subversives," "saboteurs," or "spies." Stalin would add "wrecking" to Lenin's "treason" and "subversion" list.[16] Hitler called Nazism "a voice crying 'treason.'" Hitler's SA arrested citizens as "*traitors*" and "*spies.*" Blackshirt anthems boasted, "we shall defend [Italy] against its enemies and traitors." The fascist Gabriele D'Annunzio railed in 1915 against those in the Parliament who opposed him: "Hear me—heed me—*treason* is out in the open today . . ." he cried.[17]

"Treason," "subversion," and "espionage" did their work in Czechoslovakia, Chile, and China too. Václav Havel wrote critically about the Czech state, and found he had committed a crime. It was called *disturbing the peace* and *subversion*. Havel was returned to prison in "an unsuccessful attempt to put me out of circulation, with the help of a fabricated indictment for *disturbing the peace*. . . . Like most of my colleagues," he said, "I was driven out of every position I'd once held, I was publicly branded an enemy, and I was even indicted for *subversion* (there was no trial or prison sentence.)"[18]

Do we want to be China, where prodemocracy Internet use makes one a "ruffian" or a "criminal," or Syria, where Jews are arrested as "spies"? Do we think that if the government no longer protects us, the private sector will? Google just accepted the Chinese states' restrictions on citizens' Internet use;[19] Yahoo! and AOL yielded data to the Justice Department about millions of U.S. users' searches. The ACLU is suing Boeing; it claims the company participated in rendition flights.[20]

What would Google or Yahoo! do in the United States if our government compelled these companies to comply?

Votes still count. And the only thing that will push Congress is the threat of hundreds of thousands of voters—especially Republican and swing voters—demanding that our leaders dismantle these laws or else lose their seats.

Which means that we on the left must snap out of our "it's-all-the-WTO-the-two-parties-are-the-same" torpor; and we on the right must snap out of the "if America does it, it is right" torpor as well.

We all have to reengage in an old-fashioned commitment to democratic action and believe once again in an old-fashioned notion of the Republic. We need you to help lead a democracy movement in America like the ones that have toppled repressive regimes overseas.

We can't, as a nation, switch on the metaphorical iPod and go for a run, somehow expecting a magical shift in the winds.

— CHAPTER ELEVEN —

SUBVERT *the* RULE *of* LAW

I do solemnly swear . . . that I will faithfully execute the office of President of the United States, and will to the best of my ability, preserve, protect and defend the Constitution of the United States.

PRESIDENTIAL OATH OF OFFICE

In March 2007, a scandal erupted in which eight—later, nine—U.S. attorneys were abruptly fired, perhaps with Attorney General Alberto Gonzales's knowledge. Internal Justice Department e-mails indicated that they had been targeted as being insufficiently loyal to White House policies.

New Mexico's U.S. attorney David Iglesias received an intimidating phone call from a Republican official who was upset that Iglesias hadn't prosecuted a Democratic voter registration group. Iglesias thought that there had been insufficient evidence to warrant prosecution.

In the Congressional uproar that followed, e-mails showed that while only eight prosecutors had actually been ousted, the e-mails had discussed the possibility of purging all of the U.S. attorneys. The e-mails stressed that in this eventuality, the department should stay resolute in the face of the inevitable blowback.

Congress called for subpoenas of Karl Rove and Harriet Miers. (As of this writing, Bush is simply invoking executive privilege to let him ignore the subpoenas.) But commentators were still puzzled at first: *Why* had the administration purged these attorneys, and why might it have considered purging the entire corps of U.S. attorneys?

(On April 7, 1933, in one day, recall, when Goebbels purged the civil service—specially targeting state attorneys and judges—

the baseline measure was "loyalty.")[1] How would a purge of "disloyal" U.S. attorneys in 2007, more than a year before the next national election, serve these leaders?

Remember the Alabama case of Secretary of State Worley, in which her authority to oversee the voter rolls was taken away? The Justice Department has enormous power over elections. And U.S. attorneys have the power to decide which voting registration groups to investigate and potentially prosecute.

Think again about 2008. Now think about human nature.

We assume, with our habits of democracy, that we can simply "throw the bums out" in the 2008 election.

But do people change direction so dramatically? Is it reasonable—is it really a matter of common sense—to assume that leaders who are willing to abuse signing statements; withhold information from Congress; make secret decisions; lie to the American people; use fake evidence to justify a pre-emptive war; torture prisoners; tap people's phones; open their mail and e-mail; break into their houses; and now simply ignore Congress altogether—leaders with, currently, a 29 percent approval rating—will surely say, come 2008, "The decision rests in the hands of the people. May the votes be fairly counted"?

In trusting that "the pendulum will swing" when it is time for the votes to be counted, we are like a codependent woman with an abusive boyfriend; surely next time he will do what is right.

It's a truism that the definition of madness is to do the same thing over and over and expect a different outcome. If for eight years this group has flouted other equally precious rules of the democratic game, aren't we rash to assume that this same group will see a transparent, fair election as sacrosanct? The Founders asked us to err on the side of vigilance when it came to liberty. History and current events around the world—Nigeria, Turkey, Ukraine, the Philippines—show many examples of leaders in weak or weakening democracies who were able to "co-ordinate" the civil bureaucracy with their cronies; they then tamper with the vote, and sully the outcome of elections.

If there had been a purge so that all the U.S. attorneys were Republicans in 2008, what would happen in an even somewhat close Presidential election?

Would that be America?

We in America are used to a democratic social contract in which there is agreement about the rules of the game: When Congress demands an answer, for instance, the President does not simply refuse to pick up the phone. So we keep being startled when the steps of the democratic interplay are ignored: "He can't do that!" It's time to notice that that they are playing a different game altogether.

Look at this President's use of "signing statements." The debate about this has taken place mostly among lawyers rather than among citizens, and lawyers are not tasked with explaining to ordinary Americans what that neutral, bland term *signing statements* actually means. So many of us don't get what a dramatic threat they represent.

Bush has used more signing statements than any other president. The way Bush is using signing statements essentially relegates Congress to an advisory role. This abuse lets the President choose what laws he wishes to enforce or not, overruling Congress and the people. So Americans are living under laws their representatives never passed. Signing statements put the president above the law.

So given such moves, why take for granted that this administration will uphold the rules of a free, fair election? Just because the steps of democracy have prevailed for more than 200 years does not guarantee that they will prevail tomorrow.

Fascists coming to power in a weakened democracy simply start to ignore those assumed agreements. What has happened in the past is that at a certain point in a weakening democracy, would-be dictators pretend that everything is as it should be, but simply stop responding to the will of the people and the representatives. While the nation is trying to grapple with this interim period, then such leaders deploy sudden unexpected changes that assertively upend Parliamentary protocols and expectations.

At this point, the speed of these moves itself is disorienting: It takes people some time to figure out what has happened. (In a very moving scene, Italian legislators were still frantically trying to engage in standard political negotiations with Mussolini—even as he simply waited for them to realize that the time for negotiating was over.) That psychological hangover—that delay in "getting it"—is a very dangerous time. This is the moment when action is most necessary, and this is the moment when the window is closing.

In Italy and Germany, legislators kept believing that they were still engaged in the negotiated dance of democracy—even as the militaristic march of dictatorship had already begun.

At a point in both Mussolini's and Hitler's takeovers, citizens witnessed a stunning series of quickly escalating *pronunciamentos* or *faits accomplis*. After each leader made his bids for power beyond what the Italian Parliament and the German Reichstag allowed him, each abruptly started to claim all kinds of new rights that were extra-parliamentary: the right unilaterally to go to war, to annex territory, to veto existing laws, or to overrule the judiciary.

"I am not a dictator," said Hitler in 1936. "I have only simplified democracy."[2]

At this stage, shock follows shock so quickly that the civil society institutions start to reel. At this point, in weaker democracies than ours, the police forces and the army are negotiated with. In any late shift, the final stage is the establishment of government by emergency decree or actual martial law and the leader's assertion—usually using the law to defend this assertion—that he is above the law, or that he *is* the law: the decider.

This is a classic coup: In Chile, in 1973, during a national strike, rumors circulated daily that there would be a military coup.

> Early in the day on September 11, 1973, the military left their barracks before dawn and occupied most of the radio stations. They began broadcasting marches and periodic bulletins that they were assuming control of the country. They offered [President] Allende a plane to fly out of the country and declared a national curfew that would begin at 11:00 a.m. Informed of the military's demands, Allende first told all the workers to go into the streets and defend the government, but he later changed his mind and asked them to remain alert at their factories. Allende refused to surrender, so at noon the air force bombed the national palace. Allende died. . . . The military began arresting a number of prominent government leaders while others sought refuge in foreign embassies.[3]

Some opposition members tried to resist but found they could not overcome the power of the military. The game was quickly over.

Pinochet even had a commission rewrite the Constitution; the logic of the rewrite is echoed in the U.S. Fiscal Year 2007 Defense Authorization Bill: The military could intervene on behalf of the State whenever there was a threat to the state.

Historically, the shift to martial law, or to government by emergency decree, generally takes place during a crisis. A crisis allows a would-be dictator even in a democracy to use emergency powers to restore "public order." This kind of thing won't happen in America.

But we now have a legal infrastructure in place that could support a "paper coup"—a more civilized, more marketable version of a real crackdown.

At the end of September 2006, with little outside debate, Congress passed the Fiscal Year 2007 Defense Authorization Bill—a bill that, according to journalist Major Danby, represents "a sizeable step toward weakening states' authority over their [National] Guard units." He continues: "The provision make[s] it easier for the President to declare martial law, stripping state governors of part of their authority over state National Guard units in domestic emergencies."

This guts the *Posse Comitatus* Act, the provision that the states control their own National Guard units. When the president invokes section 333, he may expand his power to declare martial law and take charge of the National Guard troops without the permission of a governor when "public order" has been lost; he can send these troops out into our streets at his direction—overriding local law enforcement authorities—during a national disaster epidemic, serious public health emergency, terrorist attack, or "other condition." He can direct these troops to disperse citizens—that is, us—and direct them to stay in their homes. The president must submit a report to Congress within 24 hours—after the fact, nonetheless.

According to this new provision, the president on his or her say-so alone can send troops from Tennessee to quell *what he or she calls* a threat to civil order—say, a peace march—in Oregon, over the objections of governors of both states.[4] The president can send what has become his or her army, not the people's, into our nation's streets and not just this president, but *any* president in the future may do this.

Vermont Senator Patrick Leahy warned, though few paid much attention, that the 2007 Defense Authorization Bill would serve to encourage a President to declare martial law.[5]

A *New York Times* editorial marked the shift—even as Americans were focused on Britney Spears's meltdown and the question of which airline serves the worst food: "A disturbing recent phenomenon in Washington is that laws that strike to the heart of American democracy have been passed in the dead of night. . . . Beyond actual insurrection, the president may now use military troops as a domestic police force in response to a natural disaster, a disease outbreak, terrorist attack or any 'other condition.'"[6]

We scarcely remember how terrified the Founders were of a standing army with the power to override the leadership of the states. The Revolutionaries knew how quickly a standing army can become bloody janissaries subduing local citizens. The Revolutionaries were certain that an American president, if he was not checked, might raise a standing army of Americans and unleash it against American citizens. This was not a far-fetched notion to them at all. They cherished their state militias as belonging to the people and responsive to the people, precisely because of this fear of a centralized American power taking up arms against them.

"If, by some turn of events, the federal government did manage to encroach on, assault, the powers of the states or vice versa, and threaten the union, the people could defeat it because the power of a republic rests in its citizens," the Federalists reassured worried fellow-citizens.[7] The Framers believed that this kind of military aggression was not possible so long as the Constitution functioned: they could not foresee the Fiscal Year 2007 Defense Authorization Bill. Nor could they have foreseen the development of private armies such as Blackwater. But their passionate debates, and the Second Amendment to the Constitution that they eventually ratified, make it clear that the Founders were desperate to protect the new nation from just what has happened while we were distracted, while we were shopping online, while we were in a Ambien-heavy sleep on the couch.

In the last phase of a fascist shift, all of the pressures that we have spelled out here tighten around ordinary citizens, working together in a kind of full-circle torsion: At this point, these pressures ensure that there is no democratic movement left. The pendulum comes to a standstill.

Of course, you will take up the Founders' banner so that can never happen.

I will say again that the United States is not vulnerable to the violent, total closing down of the system that followed Mussolini's March on Rome or Hitler's roundup of political prisoners. Our press, military, and judiciary are too independent for a scenario like that.

But there are erosions possible in all of our institutions, that could close down our experiment in democracy in ways that would look very American and familiar, but still leave us less than free.

Say, for instance, God forbid, that in a year and a half there is another terrorist attack. Say we have a President Rudolph Giuliani—or even a President Hillary Clinton. If the crisis is severe enough, the executive can and perhaps should declare a state of emergency.

But without checks and balances, history shows that any leader, of any party, will be tempted to maintain emergency powers after the crisis has subsided. In the absence of traditional checks and balances, President Hillary Clinton endangers us no less than President Giuliani. Any executive will be tempted to enforce his or her will through edict rather than submitting to the arduous process of negotiation and compromise. The Founders knew, as I wrote at the start of this primer, that excessive power was certain to corrupt equally. This danger is not about partisanship; it is about power.

Our representatives, judiciary, and press do their work today in a context in which we are "at war" in what a White House acronym calls GWOT—Global War on Terror: a war without end, on a battlefield described as the globe. So a hollowness has been expanding under the foundation of all these still-free institutions and the foundation can yield with certain kinds of pressure.

Knowing what you know now about how easy it is to close down an open society, I have to ask you to consider a series of "what-ifs." It is only if we face the "what-ifs" that we can act to make them impossible.

What if, because of a reported "threat to public order," the National Guard, now reporting directly to the President, were "backed up" with Blackwater personnel?

What if, close to the election, a Democratic voters' mobilization group were infiltrated, so that Democratic voters' names and addresses were all over the Internet? What if, as a result, you didn't believe your vote would be secret? What if some of the members of voters' groups were prosecuted for minor crimes or for immigration violations by more compliant U.S. attorneys than the nine who were purged? Those events would feel like plausible setbacks in what would still seem like home: The events would feel like an American drama, not like a beer hall putsch. But what if those kinds of events became more and more the norm?

Would that be the end of America?

What if a *Washington Post* reporter covering a story reported a classified list of detainee rights activists that had been leaked to him by a concerned civil servant? What if that reporter were charged under the 1917 Espionage Act, convicted, and sent to prison for a decade? How would it affect you to read about it the next morning?

You would read about it. If history is a guide, newspapers would continue to publish. But they would suddenly become very polite.

Would that be the end of America?

Think of the Palmer raids.

Now imagine the Palmer raids under today's legal conditions: Imagine that an equivalent of Eugene Debs—say, the head of Amnesty International—is arrested for giving a speech against torture; he is sent to a navy brig where he waits in isolation for three years to see a lawyer.

Would that be the end?

This is the United States Constitution: "The privilege of the Writ of Habeas Corpus shall not be suspended, unless when in Cases of Rebellion or Invasion the public Safety may require it."

Now listen to this exchange:

> ARLEN SPECTER: Now wait a minute, wait a minute. The Constitution says you can't take [habeas corpus] away except in the case of invasion or rebellion. Doesn't that mean you have the right of habeas corpus unless there is an invasion or rebellion?

ALBERTO GONZALES: I meant by that comment, the Constitution doesn't say, "every individual in the United States or every citizen is hereby granted or assured the right to habeas." It doesn't say that. It simply says the right of habeas corpus shall not be suspended. . . .[8]

Whatever scenario led Gonzales and his colleagues to think that one through—will *that* be the end?

GLOBAL AMERICA

I have written this book first as an American speaking to Americans. But the scenario that is unfolding has immense implications internationally.

If the United States continues on this dark road further, then truly, as James Baldwin once said, "There is no safety."[9] America's aspirations have long been global; and at our best we have offered our example as a benchmark for democracy throughout the world. But if the United States does stay this course, what "city on a hill" can shed light internationally as powerfully as we, at our best, have done?

The United States has stood for the rule of law in the past: We set a standard for other leaders, and set a point of aspiration for other citizens. If we lose that, what force on earth will stem any barbarism that any despot wishes to impose on his people?

The bureaucrats of the European Union? The fragmented voices of the United Nations?

Egyptian security forces just rounded up some of its citizens: They threw opposition leaders and a blogger in jail. When challenged, the Egyptians invoked the example of the USA PATRIOT Act.

If Fascist Germany—a medium-sized modern European state—could destabilize the globe in a matter of a few years, and it took a world war to overcome the threat, what force on earth might restrain an America that may have abandoned the rule of law—an America with its vastly greater population, wealth, and land mass; its far more sophisticated technology; its weapons systems; its already fully established global network of black-site secret prisons, and its imperial reach?

If a democratic America, with working checks and balances, often exempts itself from international agreements if its strategic interests don't coincide with international goals, would a United States led by a dictatorial regime be likely to subdue in itself any level of aggression internationally, or restrain itself from any plunder of resources that it seeks, simply because it was upsetting the rest of the world?

If we keep going down this road, the "end of America" could come, for each of us, in a different way, at a different moment. Each of us might experience a different event that would force us to look back and think: "That is how it was before—and this is the way it is now"; when we each of us alone realizes we must yield a little further our memories of a certain grace and fineness and courage that was alive in the world for a bit longer than 230 years.

Or else we can stop going down this road: We can stand our ground and fight for our nation, and take up the banner the Founders asked us to carry.

— CONCLUSION —

THE PATRIOT'S TASK

So it turns out we really are at war—a long war, a global war, a war for our civilization.

It is a war to save our democracy.

Each one of us needs to enlist. We have no one to spare.

We need citizens from across the political spectrum to carry forward the Founders' banner together. Everyone can see this movement as expressing his or her most cherished values and will frame the effort according to his or her own subculture and language. Progressives may see this "American awakening" as a liberation or, at the least, as a campaign, while conservatives may well see the same movement as "conservative" in the truest sense—a return to a stewardship of the Founders' vision. Surely "liberty" as the Founders understood it—eighteenth-century Enlightenment liberty—is the grounding of both classical conservative and classical liberal American values.

These diverse American citizens may even, in this movement, truly encounter their counterparts across the political spectrum and learn to talk to each other once again directly, as neighbors, interlocutors, and fellow patriots.

New surveillance technologies mean that today's patriots have some housekeeping to do before they can move forward effectively. This is not glamorous, but it is important to address.

Before I wrote this book, I asked an accountant to comb my tax returns, my employer records, and so on, and to identify anything that could be used against me or distorted. This process of turning an "opposition research" eye on oneself or one's organization before speaking out will have to become more common. If we are under surveillance as a nation, citizens are freer if they have disclosed their secrets to loved ones and gone over their records with a critical eye. Those in the public eye who are afraid to be forceful in opposition because of a secret they want to keep had better talk to their families or their constituencies, or their lawyers and accountants, painful as that may be in the short term. You can't fight this fight in earnest unless there is nothing left with which to blackmail you.

Some Americans, especially civil servants and members of the military, risk losing their jobs if they take up the patriot's task and speak out, or they may even risk prosecution.

Most of the rest of us? We must be willing to experience personal smears, and possibly the exposure of our secrets. Having accepted that, we all need to act and speak with courage and passion: parents, teenagers, union members, corporate leaders; the principled men and women of the military; the men and women of the FBI, CIA, and Secret Service who did not commit their lives to advance values that are un-American; those of the police forces and the National Guard who did not sign up for duty in order to suppress American rights. We need the powerful conservative Christian movement—who may recall that their own hero was a political prisoner seized by a powerful state, convicted without a trial, and tortured by military who were just doing their jobs—and we need the powerful environmental movement. We need to hold house parties, set up town halls, convene our neighbors, pass out users' guides to the Constitution, overwhelm our representatives and the Presidential candidates with demands for them to restore the rule of law.

Finally, we must stand up directly to confront those who have committed crimes against the Constitution—and hold them accountable, as the Founders trusted us to do.

Yesterday afternoon, I saw something amazing. I was trying to walk across Sixth Avenue with my little boy. But we had to pause, because dozens of colorfully dressed bicyclists—men and women and children of all races and ages—were streaming across the avenue.

It was an event organized by Critical Mass, the bike-riders' group; their goal was to show the power and benefit of tens of thousands of bike riders using city streets. I knew about this group because the Bloomberg administration had used similar Critical Mass bike rallies as a pretext to pass new laws to restrict citizens' assembly.

There were so many of them. My son and I waited, transfixed, but the numbers did not diminish: Thousands of Americans, no two of them alike, sped past us, exulting in freedom—and simply enjoying the sunshine of the day.

The power of all these Americans—moving separately yet in unison—seemed to me like the opposite of the power of the frightened and frightening masses I had been studying.

How mighty this current of citizens seemed to be once they had chosen a direction.

Bullies are cowards: Time and again, when people have awakened to danger and risen together to confront those who have sought to oppress them, citizens in their thousands have crumbled walls and broken open massive prisons. In our own nation, in times of eclipse, patriots have become rebels again and said: "No; the nation is not going down, not on my watch."

When that happens, there is no power that can hold these patriots back.

I hope this emboldens you.

Yours, Naomi
New York City
July 14, 2007

ACKNOWLEDGMENTS

I am grateful to John Brockman, Katinka Matson, Max Brockman, and Russell Weinberger for their insights about the manuscript; to the Virginia Center for the Creative Arts; to Michael Ratner at the Center for Constitutional Rights and his colleagues—Gitanjali Gutierrez, Shayana Kadidal, Wells Dixon, Emi Maclean, Bill Goodman, Jen Nessel, Esther Wang, Barbara Olshansky, Susan Hu, and Jessica Baen—for orienting me in regard to detainee issues; to Amanda Murray and David Rosenthal for their ongoing support; to Marcia Gallo of Lehman College, John Stern of John Jay College of Criminal Justice, and Zachary Heiden of the Maine Civil Liberties Union, for their valuable legal and historical readings of the manuscript; to Emily Whitfield and Barry Steinhardt of the ACLU; to my editors at the London *Guardian*, Kath Viner, Emily Wilson, and Philip Daoust, who encouraged me to publish an earlier version of this argument; to Carlton Sedgeley, Lucy LePage, and Helen Churko for their own examples of citizenship and for their insistence that this message get out; and to my colleagues Wes Boyd, Joan Blades, David Fenton, and Dr. William Haseltine of the American Freedom Campaign, for their sustained encouragement with this project and for their leadership in spearheading a citizen drive to help restore the Constitution.

Thanks to my remarkable team at Chelsea Green—editors John Barstow and Shay Totten, publisher Margo Baldwin, Mike Dyer, Kalen Landow, Erica Jong, and Emily Foote; and to Susan Devenyi, Dr. Robin Stern, Tara Bracco, David Christian, and Thomas Jackson. I am lastingly grateful to Nancy Crompton and Mary Fratini for their extraordinary commitment, dedication, and skill in the research, fact-checking, copyediting and editorial process.

I am grateful too, as always, to my beloved family, who, like all families, deserve freedom.

NOTES

INTRODUCTION

1. Mark Mazzetti, "C.I.A. Worker Says Message on Torture Got Her Fired," *New York Times,* July 22, 2006, A11.
2. R. Jeffrey Smith, "On Prosecuting Detainees: Draft Bill Waives Due Process for Enemy Combatants," *Washington Post,* July 28, 2006, A23.
3. "The Court Under Siege," Editorial, *New York Times,* July 29, 2006, A12.
4. Walter Dellinger, Editorial, "A Slip of the Pen," *New York Times,* July 31, 2006, A17.
5. Jesse Mckinley, "Blogger Jailed After Defying Court Orders," *New York Times,* August 2, 2006, A15.
6. Adam Liptak, "Government Wins Access to Reporter Phone Records," *New York Times,* August 2, 2006, A12.
7. "Strong-Arming the Vote." Editorial, *New York Times,* August 3, 2006, A20.
8. Howard Fineman, "Rove Unleashed," *Newsweek,* December 6, 2004. Available at: http://www.msnbc.msn.com/id/6597631/site/newsweek/.
9. Dana Canedy, and Dexter Filkins. "Counting the Vote: Miami-Dade County: A Wild Day in Miami, With an End to Recounting, and Democrats' Going to Court," *New York Times*, November 23, 2000, A31.
10. Nigel Williamson, "Free the Dixie Three," *The Guardian*, August 22, 2003. Available at: http://arts.guardian.co.uk/fridayreview/story/0,12102,1026475,00.html.
11. Kirk Johnson, "Colorado U. Chancellor Advises Firing Author of Sept. 11 Essay," *New York Times*, June 27, 2006, A11.
12. "ACLU Uncovers FBI Surveillance of Maine Peace Activists," ACLU Press Release, October 25, 2006. Available at: http://www.aclu.org/safefree/spyfiles/27180prs20061025.html.
13. Transcript for September 14, *NBC News, Meet the Press*, Sunday, September 7, 2003. Available at: http://www.msnbc.msn.com/id/3080244/.
14. "'We Got Him,' and Then a Call by American and Iraqi Officials for Reconciliation." Excerpts from a news conference, as recorded by Federal Document Clearing House, Inc., *New York Times*, December 15, 2003. Available at: http://www.nytimes.com/2003/12/15/politics/.
15. "JFK Airport Security Forces Woman to Drink Own Breast Milk," *USA Today/Associated Press*, August 12, 2002. Available at: http://www.usatoday.com/travel/news/2002/2002-08-09-jfk-security.htm.
16. Max Gallo, *Mussolini's Italy: Twenty Years of the Fascist Era*, trans. Charles Lam Markmann. New York: Macmillan, 1973, 117.
17. Richard J. Evans, *The Coming of the Third Reich* (New York: The Penguin Press, 2004), 341.
18. James Bovard, "Moral High Ground Not Won on Battlefield," *USA Today,* October 8, 2002. Available at: http://www.usatoday.com/news/opinion/editorials/2002-10-08-oplede_x.htm.
19. Ernestine Bradley, *The Way Home: A German Childhood, an American Life* (New York: Pantheon Books, 2005), 80.
20. Leni Riefenstahl, *Triumph des Willens (Triumph of the Will)*, Documentary, Synapse Films, 1935.
21. Reid J. Epstein, "University Warns Students of Patriot Act Disclosures: Government Can Get Medical Records," *Milwaukee Journal Sentinel*, December 17, 2004. Available at: http://www.jsonline.com/story/index.aspx?id=285173; *see also* "Reform the Patriot Act," ACLU. Available at:

http://action.aclu.org/reformthepatriotact/215.html; Richard J. Evans, *The Coming of the Third Reich*, 144–45.

22. Howard Kurtz, "Newsweek Apologizes: Inaccurate Report on Koran Led to Riots," *Washington Post*, May 16, 2005, A1.
23. Michael Ratner and Ellen Ray. *Guantánamo: What the World Should Know* (White River Junction, VT: Chelsea Green Press, 2004), 60.
24. William L. Shirer, *Berlin Diary: The Journal of a Foreign Correspondent 1934–1941* (New York: Black Dog & Leventhal Publishers, 1941), 89.
25. "Sesame Street Breaks Iraqi POWs: Heavy Metal Music and Popular American Children's Songs Are Being Used by US Interrogators to Break the Will of Their Captives in Iraq," *BBC News*, May 20, 2003. Available at: http://news.bbc.co.uk/2/hi/middle_east/3042907.stm.
26. Shirer, *Berlin Diary*, 89
27. "How U.S. Used Iraqi Wives for 'Leverage': Suspected Insurgents' Spouses Jailed to Force Husbands to Surrender," *Associated Press*, January 27, 2006. Available at: <http://www.msnbc.msn.com/id/11061831/.
28. Roy A. Medvedev, *Let History Judge: The Origins and Consequences of Stalinism*, trans. Colleen Taylor (New York: Alfred A. Knopf, 1971), 269.
29. Alan Bullock, *Hitler: A Study in Tyranny* (New York: Harper Perennial, 1962, 1971), 267, 374.
30. Vice President's Remarks at the Pentagon Observance of September 11th. Office of the Vice President, September 11, 2006. Available at: http://www.whitehouse.gov/news/releases/2006/09/20060911.html; *see also* Dr. Condoleezza Rice's Opening Remarks to Commission on Terrorist Attacks, Office of the Press Secretary, April 8, 2004. Available at: http://www.whitehouse.gov/news/releases/2004/04/20040408.html.
31. Steven Bach, *Leni: The Life and Work of Leni Riefenstahl* (New York: Alfred A. Knopf, 2007), 187.
32. Shirer, *Berlin Diary*, 324–344.
33. Ghaith Abdul-Ahad, Kael Alford, Thorne Anderson, Rita Leistner, Philip Jones Griffiths, and Phillip Robertson, *Unembedded: Four Independent Photojournalists on the War in* Iraq (White River Junction, Vermont: Chelsea Green Press, 2005), p. ii.
34. Randal C. Archibold and Jeff Kearns, "Prosecution Sees Setback at Terror Trail in California," *New York Times*, April 10, 2006, A20.
35. "California Father in Terror Case Released," *USA Today*, August 26, 2006. Available at: http://www.usatoday.com/news/nation/2006-08-25-calif-terror_x.htm.
36. Philip Shenon and Don Van Natta Jr., "A Nation Challenged: The Investigation; U.S. Says 3 Detainees May Be Tied to Hijackings," *New York Times*, November 1, 2001, A1.
37. Archibold and Kearns, ibid.
38. Eric Lichtblau, "Ex-Prosecutor in Terror Inquiry Is Indicted," *New York Times*, March 30, 2006, A18.
39. Medvedev, *Let History Judge*, 341, 354.
40. Jennifer Quinn, "British Foil Plan to Wreak Terror and Kill Thousands Over the Atlantic," *Associated Press*, printed in *The Seattle Times*, August 10, 2006. Available at: http://seattletimes.nwsource.com/html/nationworld/2003188108_londonplot10.html
41. Alan Bullock, *Hitler: A Study in Tyranny* (New York: HarperCollins, 1962, 1991), 266–67, 374.
42. Myra MacPherson, *All Governments Lie! The Life and Times of Rebel Journalist I. F. Stone* (New York: Scribner, 2006), 56.
43. Thomas Fuller, "Thai Junta Imposes Curbs on News Media," *International Herald Tribune/New York Times*,

September, 22, 2006, A13; "Wider Ban on Political Activities." *Associated Press/New York Times*, September 25, 2005, A3; "Thai Junta Revokes Ousted Prime Minister's Diplomatic Passport," *New York Times*, January 11, 2006, A13.

44. "President Bush Signs Military Commissions Act of 2006," Office of the Press Secretary, October 16, 2006. Available at: http://www.whitehouse.gov/news/releases/2006/10/20061017-1.html.
45. Author interview, October 10, 2006.

CHAPTER ONE

1. R. J. B. Bosworth, *Mussolini's Italy: Life Under Dictatorship, 1915–1945* (New York: The Penguin Press, 2006), 215.
2. Hannah Arendt, *The Origins of Totalitarianism* (New York: Harcourt, Brace, 1951), xxiii, xxvi, xxx.
3. Noam Chomsky and Edward S. Herman, *The Washington Connection and Third World Fascism* (Boston: South End Press, 1979), 28.
4. Columbia University, Paul Lagasse, Lora Goldman, Archie Hobson, and Susan R. Norton, eds., *Columbia Encyclopedia* (New York: Columbia University Press, 2001–2005), 926.
5. Joe Conason, *It Can Happen Here: Authoritarian Peril in the Age of Bush* (New York: St. Martin's Press: 2007), 22.
6. *Concise Oxford English Dictionary*, 11th ed. (London: Oxford University Press), 2006.
7. Arendt, ibid.; Carl J. Friedrich and Zbigniew K. Brzezinski, *Totalitarian Dictatorship and Autocracy* (Cambridge, MA: Harvard University Press, 1965), as cited in Eric A. Johnson and Karl-Heinz Reuband, *What We Knew: Terror, Mass Murder and Everyday Life in Nazi Germany* (New York: Basic Books, 2005), xv.
8. Johnson and Reuband, *What We Knew*, xv, xvi
9. Myra MacPherson, *All Governments Lie! The Life and Times of Rebel Journalist I. F. Stone* (New York: Scribner), 69.
10. MacPherson, *All Governments Lie!*, 115.
11. MacPherson, *All Governments Lie!*, 125; *see also* Sinclair Lewis, *It Can't Happen Here* (New York: Signet Classics, 2005).
12. Leonard W. Levy, *Origins of the Bill of Rights* (New Haven: Yale University Press, 1999), 175.
13. Alexander Hamilton, James Madison, and John Jay, *The Federalist Papers*, Clinton Rossiter, ed. (New York: The Penguin Press, 1961, 2003), 75, 103.
14. Craig Nelson, *Thomas Paine: Enlightenment, Revolution and the Birth of Modern Nations* (New York: Viking, 2006), 246.
15. Bernard Bailyn, *To Begin the World Anew: The Genius and Ambiguities of the American Founders* (New York: Alfred A. Knopf, 2003), 54–55.
16. Bailyn, *To Begin the World Anew*, 110, 111.
17. Bailyn, *To Begin the World Anew*, 123. Bailyn expanded on this theme: "Tension—networks of tensions—was the fundamental necessity for free states. The whole of the Constitution, *The Federalist* makes clear, was a great web of tensions, a system poised in tense equilibrium like the physical systems Newtonian mechanics had revealed....Pressures exerted at one point would activate rebalancing responses elsewhere; and it was in this mechanism of tense equilibria that Madison placed his hopes....," 121.
18. Denis Mack Smith, *Benito Mussolini: A Biography* (New York: Vintage Books, 1982), 21.
19. Richard J. Evans, *The Third Reich in Power* (New York: The Penguin Press, 2005), 621, 632.
20. Robert C. Tucker, *Stalin in Power: The Revolution from Above, 1928–1941*

(New York: W.W. Norton and Company), 275.

21. Dana Priest, "U.S. Instructed Latins on Executions, Torture: Manuals Used 1982–91, Pentagon Reveals" *Washington Post,* September 21, 1996, A1.
22. Max Gallo, *Mussolini's Italy: Twenty Years of the Fascist Era*, trans. Charles Lam Markmann (New York: Macmillan, 1973), 72.
23. Joseph Roth, *What I Saw: Reports from Berlin, 1920–1933* (New York: W.W. Norton and Company, 2004), 53, 179; Victor Klemperer, *I Will Bear Witness: A Diary of the Nazi Years, 1933–1941* (New York: Modern Library, 1998), 150–76.
24. Richard J. Evans, *The Coming of the Third Reich* (New York: The Penguin Press, 2004), 106–108, 145–49; Harold Donaldson Eberlein et al., *Down the Tiber and Up to Rome* (London: J. Lippincott, 1930), 107.
25. Austin Considine and Newley Purnell, "Thailand Tourists: 'Coup? What Coup?'" *New York Times*, October 8, 2006, Travel Section. Available at: http://travel.nytimes.com/2006/10/08/travel/08journeys.html.
26. Evans, *Coming of the Third Reich*, 122–129, 396–397, 403, 405.

CHAPTER TWO

1. Nat Hentoff, *The War on the Bill of Rights and the Gathering Resistance* (New York: Seven Stories Press, 2003), 11.
2. Max Gallo, *Mussolini's Italy: Twenty Years of the Fascist Era*, trans. Charles Lam Markmann (New York: Macmillan, 1973), 275.
3. "President Discusses Global War on Terror," Office of the Press Secretary, September 5, 2006. Available at: http://www.whitehouse.gov/news/releases/2006/09/20060905_4.html.
4 . Sheryl Gay Stolberg, "Buzzwords: The Decider," *New York Times,* December 24, 2006, A4.
5. Michael Gerson, "Michael Gerson on How 9/11 Changed Bush: A Former Bush Adviser on 9/11, Iraq, and The Lessons of Five Tumultuous Years—For the President and the Public," *Newsweek*, August 21–28, 2006, 59–60.
6. Richard J. Evans, *The Coming of the Third Reich* (New York: The Penguin Press, 2004), 103–112.
7. Robert O. Paxton, *The Anatomy of Fascism* (New York: Vintage Books, 2004), 37.
8. Paxton, *The Anatomy of Fascism*, 84.
9. Hannah Arendt, *The Origins of Totalitarianism* (New York: Harcourt, Brace, 1951), 424.
10. Paxton, *The Anatomy of Fascism*, 41.
11. R. J. B. Bosworth, *Mussolini's Italy: Life Under Dictatorship, 1915–1945* (New York: The Penguin Press, 2006), 141, 146.
12. Evans, *The Coming of the Third Reich*, 75.
13. Evans, *The Coming of the Third Reich*, 227.
14. Evans, *The Coming of the Third Reich*, 284–87.
15. Evans, *The Coming of the Third Reich*, 293, 298.
16. Evans, *The Coming of the Third Reich*, 80, 251, 254.
17. Evans, *The Coming of the Third Reich*, 274.
18. Leni Riefenstahl, *Triumph Des Willens (Triumph of the Will),* Documentary, Synapse Films, 1935.
19. Evans, *The Coming of the Third Reich*, 293, 298.
20. Evans, *The Coming of the Third Reich*, 310, 313–14, 332.
21. Evans, *The Coming of the Third Reich*, 311, 331–36, 349, 354.
22. Evans, *The Coming of the Third Reich*, 332.
23. Evans, *The Coming of the Third Reich*, 311, 331–36, 349, 354.
24. Anne Appelbaum, *Gulag: A History* (New York: Anchor Books, 2003), 46.

25. Barbara Miller, *The Stasi Files Unveiled: Guilt and Compliance in a Unified Germany* (New Brunswick: Transaction Publishers), 44, 49, 97.
26. John L. Rector, *The History of Chile* (New York: Palgrave Macmillan, 2003), 187.
27. Jim Stewart, "Another Terrorist Attack Coming Soon?" *CBS News*, June 5, 2006. http://www.cbsnews.com/stories/2006/06/05/terror/main1683852.shtml.
28. Jay Stanley, *The Surveillance-Industrial Complex: How the American Government Is Conscripting Businesses and Individuals in the Construction of a Surveillance Society* (New York: ACLU, 2004), 27–28.
29. Philip Shenon, "Aftereffects: Domestic Security; Former Domestic Security Aides Make a Quick Switch to Lobbying," *New York Times,* April 29, 2003, A1.
30. Author interview, December 18, 2006.
31. Author interview, January 21, 2007
32. Jay Stanley, *The Surveillance-Industrial Complex*, 28–29.

CHAPTER THREE

1. Richard J. Evans, *The Coming of the Third Reich* (New York: The Penguin Press, 2004), illustration #26; Anne Applebaum, *Gulag: A History* (New York: Anchor Books, 2003), 92–115.
2. Gail Shister, "'24' Tamps Down on Torture." *Philadelphia Inquirer*, February 15, 2007. Available at: http://www.ohio.com/mld/philly/entertainment/columnists/gail-shister/16700918.htm.
3. William Glaberson, "Plea of Guilty from a Detainee in Guantanamo." *New York Times*, March 27, 2007, A1.
4. Noam Chomsky, *The Washington Connection and Third World Fascism* (Boston: South End Press, 1979), 113.
5. Chomsky, *The Washington Connection*, 10.
6. "Egypt: Mass Arrests and Torture," Human Rights Watch, February 2005. Available at: http://hrw.org/reports/2005/egypt0205/index.htm.
7. R. J. B. Bosworth, *Mussolini's Italy: Life Under Dictatorship, 1915–1945* (New York: The Penguin Press, 2006), 241–42, 332.
8. Evans, *Coming of the Third Reich*, 317, 336, 341, 344–47, 357–58.
9. Evans, *Coming of the Third Reich*, 347.
10. Earle Rice, Jr. *The Nuremberg Trials* (San Diego, CA: Lucent Books, 1997), 31.
11. Evans, Richard J. *The Third Reich in Power* (New York: The Penguin Press, 2005), 81.
12. Evans, *The Coming of the Third Reich*, 344–49.
13. Roy A. Medvedev, *Let History Judge: The Origins and Consequences of Stalinism*, trans. Colleen Taylor (New York: Alfred A. Knopf, 1971), 279.
14. Michael Ratner, *Guantánamo: What the World Should Know* (White River Junction, VT: Chelsea Green Press, 2004), 3.
15. John Barry, Michael Hirsh, and Michael Isikoff, "The Roots of Torture," *Newsweek International,* May 24, 2004. Available at: http://www.msnbc.msn.com/id/4989481/; Nina Totenberg, *"Hamdan v. Rumsfeld:* Path to a Landmark Ruling," NPR.org, July 15, 2007. Available at: http://www.npr.org/templates/story/story.php?storyId=5751355.
16. Václav Havel, *Disturbing the Peace: A Conversation with Karel Hvizdala*, trans. Paul Wilson (New York: Alfred A. Knopf, 1990), 145.
17. Joshua Denbeaux and Mark Denbeaux, *Report on Guantánamo Detainees: A Profile of 517 Detainees through Analysis of Department of Defense Data,* April 2005. Seton Hall University, 2–3.
18. Ratner and Ray, *Guantánamo, 35.*
19. Ratner and Ray, *Guantánamo, 36.*

21. Ratner and Ray, *Guantánamo*, 36, 38, 39, 40–41, 44, 62; Applebaum, *Gulag*, 243.
22. Leonard W. Levy, *Origins of the Bill of Rights* (New Haven: Yale University Press, 1999), 74.
23. Author interview, August 13, 2006.
24. Ratner and Ray, *Guantánamo,* 25.
25. "Hamdi voices innocence, joy about reunion—Man held as 'enemy combatant' now back in Saudi Arabia." CNN, October 14, 2004. Available at: http://www.cnn.com/2004/WORLD/meast/10/14/hamdi/.
26. Nina Totenberg, "*Hamdan v. Rumsfeld:* Path to a Landmark Ruling," NPR.org, July 15, 2007. Available at: http://www.npr.org/templates/story/story.php?storyId=5751355.
27. Mike Dorning, "U.S. releases details in case against Padilla," *Chicago Tribune*, June 2, 2004. Available at: http://www.chicagotribune.com/news/nationworld/>.
28. "Profile: Jose Padilla," *BBC News*, November 22, 2005. Available at: http://news.bbc.co.uk/1/hi/world/americas/2037444.stm.
29. Ratner and Ray, *Guantánamo*, 45.
30. Naomi Klein, "A Trial for Thousands Denied Trial," *The Nation*, March 12, 2007. Available at: http://www.thenation.com/doc/20070312/klein.
31. Nina Totenberg, "U.S. Faces Major Hurdles in Prosecuting Padilla," NPR *Morning Edition*, January 3, 2007. Available at: http://www.npr.org/templates/story/story.php?storyId=6682846.
32. Karen J. Greenberg, ed., *The Torture Debate in America* (New York: Cambridge University Press, 2006), 283.
33. Greenberg, *The Torture Debate*, 312.
34. Greenberg, *The Torture Debate*, 317–57.
35. Greenberg, *The Torture Debate*, 317–57.
36. Lloyd C. Anderson, "The Detention Trilogy: Striking the Proper Balance Between National Security and Individual Liberty in an Era of Unconventional Warfare," *Whittier Law Review*, 2005. Available at: http://www.law.whittier.edu/pdfs/cstudents/wir-v27n1-anderson-abstract.pdf.
37. Author interview, September 20, 2006.
38. Applebaum, *Gulag,* 46.
39. Amy Newman, *The Nuremberg Laws* (San Diego, CA: Lucent Books, 1999), 23, 60.
40. Ratner and Ray, *Guantánamo,* 18, 24. 26.
41. Medvedev, *Let History Judge*, 258–59. For a detailed discussion of the terror in the context of party politics, see Nikolai I. Bukharin, "Crackdown on the Party," 138–145, and Carl J. Friedrich and Zbigniew K. Brzezinski. "The Model of Totalitarianism," 198–213, both articles in Robert V. Daniels, ed., *The Stalin Revolution: Foundations of Soviet Totalitarianism* (Lexington, MA: D. C. Heath and Company, 1972).
42. Medvedev. *Let History Judge*, 260.
43. Eugenia Semyonovna Ginzburg, *Journey into the Whirlwind* (San Diego, CA: Harcourt Brace & Company, 1995), 154.
44. Ratner and Ray, *Guantánamo*, 37.
45. Ratner and Ray, *Guantánamo*, 62.
46. Medvedev, *Let History Judge*, 264–65
47. "Turning Back the Clock on Rape," Editorial, *New York Times*, September 23, 2006, A10.
48. John Barry, Michael Hirsh, and Michael Isikoff, "The Roots of Torture," *Newsweek International*, May 24, 2004. Available at: http://www.msnbc.msn.com/id/4989481/.
49. Joseph Margulies, *Guantánamo and the Abuse of Presidential Power* (New York: Simon and Schuster, 2006), 133.
50. Joseph Margulies, *Guantánamo*, 99.
51. Medvedev, *Let History Judge*, 271.
52. Ginzburg, *Journey*, 79.

53. Medvedev, *Let History Judge*, 278.
54. Matthew Restall, "The Decline and Fall of the Spanish Empire?" *The William and Mary Quarterly*, Volume 64, Issue I. 2006. Available at: http://www.historycooperative.org/journals/wm/64.1/br_1.html.
55. Medvedev, *Let History Judge*, 277–78.
56. Ratner and Ray, *Guantánamo*, 39, 151.
57. Medvedev, *Let History Judge*, 276–77.
58. "After the Lawyers," Editorial, *New York Times*, April 27, 2007, A26.
59. Margulies, *Guantánamo*, 163–64.
60. Ginzburg, *Journey*, 170–72.
61. Seymour M. Hersh, "Torture at Abu Ghraib," *New Yorker*, May 10, 2004. Available at: http://www.newyorker.com/archive/2004/05/10/040510fa_fact.
62. Steven H. Miles, *Oath Betrayed: Torture, Medical Complicity, and the War on Terror* (New York: Random House, 2006).
63. Michael Isikoff and Stuart Taylor Jr., "The Gitmo Fallout," *Newsweek*, July 17, 2006, 22–25.
64. Alan Bullock, *Hitler: A Study in Tyranny* (New York: HarperCollins, 1962, 1991), 374–75.
65. Nick Hawton, "Hunt for CIA 'Black Site' in Poland," *BBC News*, December 28, 2006. Available at: http://news.bbc.co.uk/2/hi/europe/6212843.stm.
66. Nat Hentoff, "Our Own Nuremberg Trials," *Village Voice*, December 20–26, 2006, 14.
67. Patrick Quinn, "U.S. War Prisons Become Legal Vacuum for 14,000," *Associated Press*, September 18, 2006. Available at: http://www.king5.com/sharedcontent/iraq/topstories/091806ccwcIraqPrisoners.1f7e92fd.html.
68. "U.S.: Soldiers Tell of Detainee Abuse in Iraq," Human Rights Watch, July 23, 2006. Available at: http://hrw.org/english/docs/2006/07/19/usint13767.htm.
69. Applebaum, *Gulag*, 9.
70. Evans, *Third Reich in Power*, 136–37.
71. Evans, *Third Reich in Power,* 68–70, 453.
72. Peter Noel, "The Louima Millions," *Village Voice*, July 18–24, 2001.
73. Alfred W. McCoy, "The Myth of the Ticking Time Bomb," *The Progressive*, October, 2006. Available at: http://www.progressive.corg/mag_mccoy1006; Alfred W. McCoy, A question of Torture (New York: Henry Holt, 2006), 111.
74. Myra MacPherson, *All Governments Lie! The Life and Times of Rebel Journalist I. F. Stone* (New York: Scribner, 2006), 272.
75. Ratner and Ray, *Guantánamo*, 43.
76. Author interview, January 27, 2007.
77. Adam Liptak, "Judge Hears Arguments on Federal Spying Program," *New York Times*, September 6, 2006, A14.
78. Alexander Hamilton, James Madison, John Jay, *The Federalist Papers*, ed. by Clinton Rossiter (New York: The Penguin Press, 1961, 2003), 498.

CHAPTER FOUR

1. Jeremy Scahill, *Blackwater: The Rise of the World's Most Powerful Mercenary Army* (New York: Nation Books, 2007), xviii–xix.
2. Scahill, *Blackwater*, xix.
3. Scahill, *Blackwater,* 72–73.
4. Scott Shane, "C.I.A. Contractor Guilty in Beating of Afghan Who Later Died," *New York Times*, August 18, 2006, A8.
5. Scahill, *Blackwater*, xx–xxi.
6. Scahill, *Blackwater*, 186, 190–99, 200, 202.
7. Scahill, *Blackwater*, 327–29
8. Robert Young Pelton, *Licensed to Kill: Hired Guns in the War on Terror* (New York: Crown Publishers, 2006), 31.
9. Pelton, *Licensed to Kill*, 2.
10. Pelton, *Licensed to Kill*, 4–5.
11. Sidney Blumenthal, *How Bush Rules* (Princeton, New Jersey: Princeton University Press, 2006), 2.
12. Don Van Natta, Jr., "The 2000

Campaign: The Florida Vote; Democrats Tell of Problems at the Polls Across Florida," *New York Times*, November 10, 2000, A26.

13. Richard J. Evans, *The Coming of the Third Reich* (New York: The Penguin Press, 2004), 274.
14. R. J. B. Bosworth, *Mussolini's Italy: Life under Dictatorship, 1915–1945* (New York: The Penguin Press, 2006), 95.
15. William L. Shirer, *Berlin Diary: The Journal of a Foreign Correspondent 1934–1941* (New York: Black Dog & Leventhal Publishers, 1941), 90.
16. Kirk Johnson, "Man Sues Secret Service Agent Over Arrest After Approaching Cheney and Denouncing War," *New York Times*, October 4, 2006, A22.
17. Gallo, *Mussolini's Italy*, 41–45.
18. Evans, *Coming of the Third Reich*, 181–82, 191.
19. Evans, *Coming of the Third Reich*, 230.
20. Eric A. Johnson and Karl-Heinz Reuband, *What We Knew: Terror, Mass Murder and Everyday Life in Nazi Germany* (New York: Basic Books, 2005), 54.

CHAPTER FIVE

1. Nat Hentoff, *The War on the Bill of Rights and the Gathering Resistance* (New York: Seven Stories Press, 2003), 75.
2. Barbara Miller, *The Stasi Files Unveiled: Guilt and Compliance in a Unified Germany* (New Brunswick: Transaction Publishers), 2.
3. Author interview, August 2006.
4. Nicholas D. Kristof and Sheryl WuDunn, *China Wakes: The Struggle for the Soul of a Rising Power* (New York: Vintage Books, 1995), 49.
5. Eric Lichtblau and James Risen, "Bush Lets U.S. Spy on Callers Without Courts," *New York Times*, December 16, 2005, A1.
6. James Risen and Eric Lichtblau, "Bank Data Sifted in Secret by U.S. to Block Terror," *New York Times*, June 23, 2006, A1.
7. Author interview, August 13, 2006.
8. David Cunningham, *There's Something Happening Here—The New Left, the Klan, and FBI Counterintelligence* (Berkeley: University of California Press, 2004), 2.
9. R. J. B. Bosworth, *Mussolini's Italy: Life under Dictatorship, 1915–1945* (New York: The Penguin Press, 2006), 233.
10. Bosworth, *Mussolini's Italy*, 310.
11. William L. Shirer, *Berlin Diary: The Journal of a Foreign Correspondent 1934–1941* (New York: Black Dog & Leventhal Publishers, 1941), 469.
12. Richard J. Evans, *The Coming of the Third Reich* (New York: The Penguin Press, 2004), 229.
13. Evans, Coming of the Third Reich, 143–144.
14. Shirer, *Berlin Diary*, 448.
15. Barbara Miller, *The Stasi Files Unveiled: Guilt and Compliance in Unified Germany* (New Brunswick: Transaction Publishers, 2004), 3–25.
16. Eric A. Johnson and Karl-Heinz Reuband, *What We Knew: Terror, Mass Murder, and Everyday Life in Nazi Germany* (New York: Basic Books, 2005), 181.
17. Václav Havel, *Disturbing the Peace: A Conversation with Karel Hvizdala*, trans. Paul Wilson (New York: Alfred A. Knopf, 1990), xi.
18. Kristof and WuDunn. ibid., 22.

CHAPTER SIX

1. Roy A. Medvedev, *Let History Judge: The Origins and Consequences of Stalinism*, trans. Colleen Taylor (New York: Alfred A. Knopf, 1971), 352–54.
2. Richard J. Evans, *The Coming of the Third Reich* (New York: The Penguin Press, 2004), 403.
3. John L. Rector, *The History of Chile* (New York: Palgrave Macmillan, 2003), 202.

4. David Cunningham, *There's Something Happening Here: The New Left, The Klan, and FBI Counterintelligence* (Berkeley: University of California Press, 2004), 109.
5. Mark Schlosberg, "The State of Surveillance: Government Monitoring of Political Activity in Northern & Central California," ACLU of Northern California, July 2006. Available at: http://www.aclunc.org/issues/govern ment_surveillance/the_state_of_sur veillance.shtml.
6. Joe Conason, *It Can Happen Here: Authoritarian Peril in the Age of Bush* (New York: St. Martin's Press: 2007), 192–93.
7. Eric Lichtblau and Mark Mazzetti, "Military Documents Hold Tips on Antiwar Activities," *New York Times*, November 21, 2006, A18.
8. Author interview, May 9, 2007, Center for Constitutional Rights.
9. Jim Dwyer, Jim. "City Asks Court Not to Unseal Police Spy Files," *New York Times*, March 26, 2007, B1.
10. Mark Bushnell, "The Minister Was Jailed for Anti-war Beliefs," *Times Argus Sunday Magazine*, December 12, 2004. Available at: http://www.times argues.com/apps/pbsc.d11/article?AI D=2004121/NEWS/412120306/1013; Geoffrey R. Stone, *War and Liberty: An American Dilemma, 1790 to the Present* (New York: W.W. Norton, 2007), 55.
11. "Taxing an Unfriendly Church," Editorial, *New York Times*, November 22, 2005, A22.
12. Stephanie Strom, "Group Seeks I.R.S. Inquiry into 2 Ohio Churches Accused of Improper Campaigning," *New York Times*, January 16, 2006, A9.
13. "Activist Sheehan Arrested in House Gallery," CNN.com. February 1, 2006. Available at: http://www.cnn.com/ 2006/POLITICS/01/31/sheehan. arrest/.
14. Cornelia Dean, "A Man, a Plan, a Dam. Then, an FBI Call," *New York Times*, August 22, 2006, A15.

CHAPTER SEVEN

1. Sara Kehaulani Goo, "Sen. Kennedy Flagged by No-Fly List," *Washington Post,* August 20, 2004, A01.
2. Sara Kehaulani Goo, "Cat Stevens Held after D.C. Flight Diverted." *Washington Post*, September 22, 2004, A10.
3. Bob Cuddy, "Caught in the Backlash: Stories from Northern California," ACLU of Northern California, September 11, 2002, 8.
4. "ACLU of Massachusetts Challenges Use of Behavioral Profiling at Logan Airport," ACLU. Available at: <www.aclu.org/safefree/general/ 18765prs20041110.html.
5. Author interview, August 31, 2006.
6. Mark Graber, "Another Enemy of the People?" Balkinization Blog, April 8, 2007. Available at: http://balkin. blogspot.com/2007/04/another-enemy-of-people.html.
7. "Unlikely Terrorists on No-Fly List," *CBS News*, October 8, 2006. Available at: http://cbsnews.com/stories/2006/ 10/10/60minutes.
8. Timothy Williams, "Aide Detained at Kennedy en Route to Venezuela," *New York Times*, September 24, 2006, A37.
9. "Frequently Asked Questions About the No-Fly List," ACLU. September 22, 2005. Available at: http://www. aclu-wa.org/detail.cfm?id=274.
10. *CBS,* ibid.
11. Eric Lichtblau, "Democrats Set to Press Bush on Privacy and Terrorism," *New York Times*, December 7, 2006, A37.
12. Scott Shane, "Canadian to Remain on U.S. Terrorist Watch List," *New York Times*, January 23, 2007, A11; author interview May 9, 2007, Center for Constitutional Rights.
13. Myra MacPherson, *All Governments Lie! The Life and Times of Rebel*

Journalist I. F. Stone. New York: Scribner, 2006, 339.

14. William L. Shirer, *Berlin Diary: The Journal of a Foreign Correspondent 1934–1941* (New York: Black Dog & Leventhal Publishers, 1941), 143–44.
15. Chris Plante, "U.S. Army Muslim chaplain arrested," *CNN*, September 22, 2003. Available at: <http://www.cnn.com/2003/US/09/20/chaplain.arrest.
16. Laura Parker, "The Ordeal of Chaplain Yee," *USA Today*, May 16, 2004. Available at: http://www.usatoday.com/news/nation/2004-05-16-yee-cover_x.htm.
17. Damien Cave, "The Struggle for Iraq: U.S. Jailer in Iraq Admits Mistakes, Investigator Says," *New York Times*, May 2, 2007, A10; "Senior U.S. officer in Iraq accused of aiding the enemy," *CBS News*, April 26, 2007.
18. "Former Army Chaplain Is Stopped at Border," *New York Times*, July 24, 2006; Victor Klemperer, *I Will Bear Witness: A Diary of the Nazi Years, 1933–1941* (New York: Modern Library, 1999), 276.
19. Eric A. Johnson and Karl-Heinz Reuband, *What We Knew: Terror, Mass Murder and Everyday Life in Nazi Germany* (New York: Basic Books, 2005), 290, 291.
20. Evans, *Third Reich in Power*, 603.
21. Rector, *History of Chile*, 188.
22. "FBI apologizes to lawyer in bombing case." *Associated Press/MSNBC*, May 25, 2004. Available at: http://www.msnbc.msn.com/id/5053007.
23. Dan Eggen, "U.S. Settles Suit Filed by Ore. Lawyer," *Washington Post*, November 30, 2006, A03.
24. Leonard W. Levy, *Origins of the Bill of Rights* (New Haven: Yale University Press, 1999), 153–57.
25. Mark Kurlansky, *1968: The Year That Rocked the World* (New York: Random House, 2005), 339.
26. John L. Rector, *The History of Chile* (New York: Palgrave Macmillan, 2003), 208.
27. Diane Cardwell, "In Court Papers, A Political Note on '04 Protests," *New York Times*, July 31, 2006, B1.
28. Christopher Dunn and Donna Lieberman, "License to Stroll," *New York Times,* August 13, 2006, 14:11.

CHAPTER EIGHT

1. "Science Under Siege: The Bush Administration's Assault on Academic Freedom and Scientific Inquiry," ACLU, June 2005, 29, 31.
2. Richard J. Evans, *The Coming of the Third Reich* (New York: The Penguin Press, 2004), 426.
3. Gunther Neske and Emil Kettering, eds., *Martin Heidegger and National Socialism* (New York: Paragon House, 1990), 5–13.
4. "'Intellectual Diversity': Slogan for the New McCarthyism" Reprinted from the Community College Perspective, May 2005. Available at: http://www.cft.org/councils/ccc/news/santarosared.html.
5. Michelle York, "Professor Is Assailed by Legislature and Vandals," *New York Times*, February 3, 2005, B6.
6. Kirk Johnson, "Colorado U. Chancellor Advises Firing Author of Sept. 11 Essay," *New York Times*, June 27, 2006, A11.
7. Gretchen Ruethling, "A Skeptic on 9/11 Prompts Questions on Academic Freedom," *New York Times*, August 1, 2006, A11.
8. Stanley Fish, "Conspiracy Theories 101," *New York Times*, July 23, 2006, 4:13.
9. Heidegger, ibid.
10. R. J. B. Bosworth, *Mussolini's Italy: Life under Dictatorship, 1915–1945* (New York: The Penguin Press, 2006), 243.
11. Evans, *Coming of the Third Reich*, 416; Jean-Michel Plamier, *Weimar in Exile: The Anti-Fascist Emigration in Europe*

and America (London: Verso, 2006), 1–47.

12. Evans, *Coming of the Third Reich*, Illustration #28.
13. Evans, *Coming of the Third Reich*, 419, 422–23, 425, 568.
14. Palmier, *Weimar in Exile*, 44.
15. John L. Rector, *The History of Chile* (New York: Palgrave Macmillan, 2003), 200–02.
16. Nicholas D. Kristof and Sheryl WuDunn, *China Wakes: The Struggle for the Soul of a Rising Power* (New York: Vintage Books, 1995), 27.
17. Warren St. John, "The Backlash Grows Against Celebrity Activists," *New York Times*, March 23, 2003, 9:1.
18. Theo Emery, "In Nashville, Sounds of Political Uprising From the Left," *New York Times*, August 19, 2006. Available at: http://www.nytimes.com/2006/08/19/washington/19nashville.html?ex=1183780800&en=fea052dbd5163444&ei=5070.
19. John Schwartz and Geraldine Fabrikant, "War Puts Radio Giant on the Defensive," *New York Times*, Mar 31, 2003, C1.
20. Michael Moore, "Sicko is Completed and We're Off to Cannes!" May 17, 2007. Available at: www.michaelmoore.com/words/message/index.php?messageDate=2007-05-17.
21. Evans, *Coming of the Third Reich*, 398; Palmier, *Weimar in Exile*, 113.
22. Rector, *History of Chile*, 22.
23. Myra MacPherson, *All Governments Lie! The Life and Times of Rebel Journalist I. F. Stone* (New York: Scribner, 2006, 302–03.
24. Victor Klemperer, *I Will Bear Witness: A Diary of the Nazi Years, 1933–1941*, trans. Martin Chalmers (New York: The Modern Library, 1998), 19.
25. David Johnston and Scott Shane, "C.I.A. Dismisses a Senior Official Over Data Leaks," *New York Times*, April 22, 2006, A1.
26. Scott Shane, "Criminal Inquiry Opens Into Leak in Eavesdropping," *New York Times*, December 31, 2005, A1.
27. David Johnston and Neil A. Lewis, "Lawyer Says Military Tried to Coerce Detainee's Plea," *New York Times*, June 16, 2005, A25.
28. "The Cost of Doing Your Duty," Editorial, *New York Times*, October 11, 2006, A26.
29. "Apology Not Accepted," Editorial, *New York Times*, January 19, 2007, A22; Amy Newman, *The Nuremberg Laws: Institutionalized Anti-Semitism* (San Diego: Lucent Books, 1970), 18–19.

CHAPTER NINE

1. Joseph C. Wilson, 4th, "What I Didn't Find in Africa," *New York Times,* July 6, 2003, 4:9.
2. Eric Boehlert, "Swift Boat flacks Attack CBS," *Salon.com*, September 10, 2004. Available at: http://dir.salon.com/story/news/feature/2004/09/10/forgery/index.html.
3. "Politicizing Public Broadcasting," Editorial, *New York Times*, May 4, 2005, A22.
4. Elizabeth Jensen, "PBS Firing of the Host on a Show for Children Draws Protest," *New York Times*, August 5, 2006, A15, A20.
5. Fintan Dunne, "Pentagon Threatens to Kill Independent Reporters in Iraq," March 10, 2003. Available at: http://www.breakfornews.com/news/kate_adie030310.htm.
6. "Reporters Without Borders Accuses U.S. Military of Deliberately Firing at Journalists," Posted on Reporters Without Borders: For Press Freedom, April 8, 2003. Available at: http://www.rsf.org/article.php3?id_article=5975.
7. Robert Fisk,"No Wonder al-Jazeera was a target," *The Independent*, November 26, 2005. Available at: http://www.robert-fisk.com/articles548.htm.
8. "EXCLUSIVE: Al Jazeera Reporters

Give Bloody First Hand Account of April '04 U.S. Siege of Fallujah, interview posted on *Democracy Now!* February 22, 2006. Available at: http://www.democracynow.org/article.pl?sid=06/02/22/1434210.

9. Kevin Maguire, "Exclusive: Bush Plot to Bomb His Arab Ally." *Daily Mirror*, November 22, 2005. Available at: http://www.mirror.co.uk.news/
10. Jeremy Scahill, "Did Bush Really Want to Bomb Al Jazeera?" *The Nation*, November 23, 2005. Available at: http://www.thenation.com/doc/20051212/scahill.
11. Nicholas Kristof, "Sami's Shame, and Ours," *New York Times*, October 17, 2006, A21.
12. "Trial for Detained CBS News Cameraman Set for April," *CBS News*, March 2, 2006. Available at: http://www.cbsnews.com/blogs/2006/03/22/publiceye/.
13. "CBS freelance cameraman shot and wounded by US soldiers," Reporters Without Borders, April 6, 2005. Available at: http://www.rsf.org/article.php3?id_article=13118.
14. "Iraqi Cameraman for CBS Faces Trial," *CBS News*, March 22, 2006. Available at: http://www.cbsnews.com/stories/2006/03122/Iraq.
15. "CBS Cameraman Acquitted in Iraq Panel Rules There Was a Lack of Evidence a Year after Arrest," *CBS News*, April 5, 2006. Available at: http://www.cbsnews.com/stories/2006/04/05/iraq/main1472263.shtml
16. "U.S. Holds AP Photographer in Iraq," *CBS News*, September 18, 2006.
17. C. J. Chivers, "Journalist Critical of Chechen War Is Shot Dead in Moscow," *New York Times*, October 8, 2006, sec. 1, p. 16.
18. Sebnem Arsu, "Editor Who Spoke for Turkey's Ethnic Armenians Is Slain," *New York Times*, January 20, 2007, A3.
19. "Army: Milblogging Is 'Therapy,' Media Is 'Threat'," Wired Blog Network, May 2, 2007. Available at: http://blog.wired.com/defense/2007/05/army_milbloggin.html.
20. Paul McLeary, "Is This What the Army Thinks of Us? A new Army manual paints American reporters as a national security threat," *Columbia Journalism Review*. May 3, 2007. Available at: <http://www.cjr.org/politics/is_this_what_the_army_thinks_o.php?.
21. "Protecting Reporters' Phone Records," Editorial, *New York Times*, November 29, 2006, A28.
22. Tom Socca, "Off the Record," *New York Observer*, September 8, 2006, p. 6.
23. Michael Calderone, "Times Studies How to Shake Feds: Disposable Phones, Erasable Notes: 'Act Like a Drug Dealer,'" *The New York Observer*, September 17, 2006. Available at: http://www.observer.com/node/39419.
24. Greg Palast, "Palast Charged with Journalism in the First Degree," September 11, 2006. Available at: <http://www.gregpalast.com/palast-charged-with-journalism-in-the-first-degree.
25. Max Gallo, *Mussolini's Italy: Twenty Years of the Fascist Era*, trans. Charles Lam Markmann (New York: Macmillan, 1964), 38.
26. R. J. B. Bosworth, *Mussolini's Italy: Life under Dictatorship, 1915–1945* (New York: The Penguin Press, 2006), 217–18.
27. Bosworth, *Mussolini's Italy*, 220.
28. Richard J. Evans, *The Third Reich in Power* (New York: The Penguin Press, 2005), 153.
29. Evans. *Third Reich in Power*, 407; Ralf Georg Reuth, *Goebbels* (New York: Harcourt Brace & Co.), 75–192.
30. Nicholas D. Kristof and Sheryl WuDunn, *China Wakes: The Struggle for the Soul of a Rising Power* (New York: Vintage, 1995), 25–26.
31. Elisabeth Bumiller, "Keepers of Bush Image Lift Stagecraft to New Heights,"

New York Times, May 16, 2003, A1; Leni Riefenstahl, *Triumph des Willens (Triumph of the Will)*, 1935, Documentary, Synapse Films, 1935; Ray Müller, *The Wonderful, Horrible Life of Leni Riefenstahl*, Channel Four Films, Germany, 1994; Steven Bach, *The Life and Work of Leni Reifenstahl* (New York: Alfred A. Knopf, 2007), 116.

32. Evans, *Coming of the Third Reich*, 168.
33. George Orwell, *Animal Farm* (New York: Harcourt Brace, 1997), 57.
34. William L. Shirer, *Berlin Diary: The Journal of a Foreign Correspondent 1934–1941* (New York: Black Dog & Leventhal Publishers, 1941), 269.
35. Evans, *Third Reich in Power*, 664–71.
36. John L. Rector, *The History of Chile* (New York: Palgrave Macmillan, 2003), 187.
37. Frank Rich, *The Greatest Story Ever Sold: The Decline and Fall of Truth From 9/11 to Katrina* (New York: The Penguin Press, 2006), 229–307.
38. Howard Kurtz, "Administration Paid Commentator: Education Dept. Used Williams to Promote 'No Child' Law." *Washington Post*, January 8, 2005, A1.
39. Katharine Q. Seelye, "Miami Publisher Steps Down Over Payments to Reporters," *New York Times*, October 4, 2006, A16.
40. George Orwell, "Looking Back on the Spanish War," in *Essays by George Orwell*. Available at: http://www.george-orwell.org/Looking_Back_On_The_Spanish_War/0.html.
41. Jess McKinley, "Three from Clinton Administration Urge Disney to Cancel or Revise 9/11 Mini-Series," *New York Times*, September 7, 2006, A27.
42. "Media reports fail to probe 9-11 Commission chairman Kean's role with ABC's factually flawed path to 9/11 miniseries," *Media Matters*, September 7, 2006. Available at: http://mediamatters.org/items/200609070007.
43. Don Kaplan and David K. Li, "Secrets of First 9/11 Miniseries," *New York Post*, July 28, 2005.
44. Orwell, *Animal Farm*, 47–48.

CHAPTER TEN

1. Eric A. Jones, *Urbanization and Crime: Germany, 1871–1914*. Cambridge: Cambridge University Press, 1995, 27; Victor Klemperer, *I Will Bear Witness: A Diary of the Nazi Years, 1933–1941*, trans. Martin Chalmers (New York: The Modern Library, 1998), 77, 130, 190; Roy A. Mededev, *Let History Judge: The Origins and Consequences of Stalinism* (New York: Alfred A. Knopf, 1971), 346–47.
2. Klemperer, ibid., 79–120.
3. Ann Coulter, *Treason: Liberal Treachery from the Cold War to the War on Terrorism* (New York: Random House, 2003), 203.
4. Coulter, *Treason*, 257–58.
5. Deroy Murdock, "Gray Lady's Serial Spills," *National Review Online*, July 6, 2006. Available at: http://article.nationalreview.com/.
6. Brian Maloney, "Still Going," *The Radio Equalizer*, July 10, 2006. Available at: http://radioequalizer.blogspot.com/2006_07_01_archive.html.
7. Medvedev, *Let History Judge*, 175–78.
8. Maloney, ibid.
9. Murdock, ibid.
10. Dan Eggen and Jerry Markton, "2 Senior AIPAC Employees Ousted: FBI Investigating if Pair Gave Classified Information to Israel," *Washington Post*, April 21, 2005, A8.
11. Eric Lichtblau, "American in al-Qaeda Tapes Accused of Treason," *New York Times*, October 12, 2006, A22.
12. Myra MacPherson, *All Governments Lie! The Life and Times of Rebel Journalist I. F. Stone* (New York: Scribner, 2006), 54–55.
13. MacPherson, *All Governments Lie!*, 57.

14. MacPherson, *All Governments Lie!*, 58–59.
15. "ACLU Letter to Congress Urging Opposition to the Animal Enterprise Act, S. 1926 and H.R. 4239," ACLU, March 6, 2006. Available at http://www.aclu.org/freespeech/gen/25620leg20060306.html.
16. Applebaum, *Gulag*, 46.
17. Max Gallo, *Mussolini's Italy: Twenty Years of the Fascist Era*, trans. Charles Lam Markmann (New York: Macmillan, 1973), 43.
18. Václav Havel, *Disturbing the Peace: A Conversation with Karel Hvizdala*, trans. Paul Wilson (New York: Alfred A. Knopf, 1990), 120, 143.
19. Jim Hopkins, "Bill would keep servers out of China," *USA Today*, February 12, 2006. Available at: http://www.usatoday.com/money/world/2006-02-12-china-net_x.htm.
20. ACLU Sues Boeing Subsidary for Participating in CIA Kidnapping and Torture Flights." ACLU, May 30, 2007. Available at http://www.aclu.org/safefree/torture/29920prs20070530.html.

CHAPTER ELEVEN

1. Richard J. Evans, *The Third Reich in Power* (New York: The Penguin Press, 2005), 14–15.
2. Victor Klemperer, *I Will Bear Witness: A Diary of the Nazi Years, 1933–1941* (New York: Modern Library, 1998), 157.
3. John L. Rector, *The History of Chile* (New York: Palgrave Macmillan, 2003), 182.
4. Major Danby, "Bush Guts Posse Comitatus, Grabs National Guard." *News From Underground*, Wednesday, October 18, 2006.
5. Patrick Leahy, "Remarks of Sen. Patrick Leahy, National Defense Authorization Act For Fiscal Year 2007, Conference Report, Congressional Record," September 29, 2006. Available at: http://leahy.senate.gov/press/200609/092906b.html.
6. "Making Martial Law Easier," Editorial, *New York Times*, February 19, 2007, A14
7. Levy, *Origin of the Bill of Rights*, 193.
8. Available at: http://jurist.law.pitt.edu/monitor/2007/01/gonzales-surveillance-authorization.php *See also*: http://thinkprogress.org/2007/01/19/gonzales-habeas/.
9. Fred L. Stanley and Louis H. Pratt, eds., *Conversations with James Baldwin* (Jackson: University Press of Mississippi, 1989), 78.

BIBLIOGRAPHY

Abdul-Ahad, Ghaith, Kael Alford, Thorne Andersen, and Rita Leistner. *Unembedded: Four Independent Photojournalists on the War in Iraq*. White River Junction, VT: Chelsea Green Publishing, 2005.

Applebaum, Anne. *Gulag: A History*. New York: Anchor Books, 2003.

Arendt, Hannah. *The Origins of Totalitarianism*. New York: Harcourt, Brace, 1951.

Ash, Timothy Garton. *The File: A Personal History*. New York: Random House, 1997.

Auden, W. H. *Collected Poems*. Reprint. Edward Mendelson (ed.). New York: Vintage Books, 1991.

Bach, Steven. *Leni: The Life and Work of Leni Riefenstahl*. New York: Knopf, 2007.

Bailyn, Bernard. *To Begin the World Anew: The Genius and Ambiguities of the American Founders*. New York: Albert A. Knopf, 2003.

Benedict, Michael Les. *The Blessings of Liberty: A Concise History of the Constitution of the United States*. Lexington, MA: D. C. Heath and Co., 1996.

Bosworth, R. J. B., *Mussolini's Italy: Life Under Dictatorship, 1915-1945*, New York: The Penguin Press, 2006.

Brookhiser, Richard. *Alexander Hamilton, American*. New York: Simon and Schuster, 1999.

Bullock, Alan. *Hitler: A Study in Tyranny*. New York: HarperCollins, 1962, 1991.

Chomsky, Noam. *9-11*. New York: Seven Stories Press, 2001.

Collins, Gail. *America's Women: 400 Years of Dolls, Drudges, Helpmates and Heroines*. New York: William Morrow, 2003.

Conason, Joe. *It Can't Happen Here: Authoritarian Peril in the Age of Bush*. New York: St. Martin's Press, 2007.

Cunningham, David. *There's Something Happening Here: The New Left, The Klan, and FBI Counterintelligence*. Berkeley: University of California Press, 2004.

Daniels, Robert V. *The Stalin Revolution: Foundations of Soviet Totalitarianism*. Lexington, MA: D.C. Heath and Company, 1972.

Dawidowicz, Lucy S. *The War Against the Jews, 1933-1945*. New York: Holt, Rhinehart and Winston, 1975.

Ellis, Joseph J. *Founding Brothers: The Revolutionary Generation*. New York: Vintage, 2002.

Eberlein, Harold Donaldson, Geoffrey J. Marks, and Frank A.Wallis. *Down the Tiber and Up to Rome*. Philadelphia: J. B. Lippincott Company, 1930.

Evans, Richard J. *The Coming of the Third Reich*. New York: The Penguin Press, 2004.

Evans, Richard J. *The Third Reich in Power*. New York: The Penguin Press, 2005.

Franklin, Benjamin. *Autobiography and Other Writings*. Ormond Seavey (ed.). Oxford, U.K.: Oxford University Press, 1993.

Gallo, Max. *Mussolini's Italy: Twenty Years of the Fascist Era*. Trans. Charles Lam Markmann. New York: Macmillan Publishing Company, Inc., 1964.

Gibbs, Philip. *European Journey, Being the Narrative of a Journey in France, Switzerland, Italy, Hungary, Austria, Germany and the Saar, in the Spring and Summer of 1934*. New York: The Literary Guild, 1934.

Glasser, Ira. *Visions of Liberty: The Bill of Rights for all Americans*. New York: Arcade Publishing, 1991.

Goodman, Amy. *The Exception to the Rulers: Exposing Oily Politicians, War Profiteers, and the Media That Love Them*. New York: Hyperion, 2004.

Grandin, Greg. *Empire's Workshop: Latin America, The United States and the Rise of the New Imperialism*. New York: Holt, 2006.

Green, James. *Death in the Haymarket: A Story of Chicago, The First Labor Movement and the Bombing That Divided Gilded Age America*. New York: Anchor Books, 2007.

Greenwald, Glenn. *How Would a Patriot Act? Defending American Values from a President Run Amok.* San Francisco: Working Assets Publishing, 2006.

Halberstam, David. *The Fifties.* New York: Fawcett Columbine, 1993.

Halle, Louis J. *The Cold War as History*. New York: Harper & Row, 1967.

Hamilton, Alexander, James Madison, and John Jay, *The Federalist Papers*. Clinton Rossiter (ed.). New York: Signet, 1961, 2003.

Harris, Sam. *Letter to a Christian Nation*. New York: Alfred A. Knopf, 2006.

Hochman, Jiri, ed. and trans., *Hope Dies Last: The Autobiography of Alexander Dubcek.* New York: Kodansha International, 1993.

Holtzman, Elizabeth, with Cynthia L. Cooper. *The Impeachment of George W. Bush: A Practical Guide for Concerned Citizens*. New York: Nation Books, 2006.

Isaacson, Walter (ed.). *A Benjamin Franklin Reader*. New York: Simon and Schuster, 2003.

Jensen, Derrick, and George Draffan. *Welcome to the Machine: Science, Surveillance, and the Culture of Control.* White River Junction, VT: Chelsea Green Publishing, 2004.

Johnson, Chalmers. *Nemesis: The Last Days of the American Republic.* New York: Holt, 2006.

Johnson, Eric A., and Karl-Heinz Reuband. *What We Knew: Terror, Mass Murder and Everyday Life in Nazi Germany*, New York: Basic Books, 2005.

Kessler, Count Harry. *Berlin in Lights: The Diaries of Count Harry Kessler, 1918–1937*. Ian Buruma (ed.). Trans. Charles Kessler. New York: Grove Press, 1961.

Klemperer, Victor. *I Will Bear Witness: A Diary of the Nazi Years, 1933–1941*. Trans. Martin Chalmers. New York: The Modern Library, 1998.

Koren, Yehuda, and Eilat Negev. *Lover of Unreason: Assia Wevill, Sylvia Plath's Rival and Ted Hughes's Doomed Love.* New York: Carroll and Graf Publishers, 2006.

Korda, Michael. *Journey to a Revolution: A Personal Memoir and History of the Hungarian Revolution of 1956*. New York: HarperCollins, 2006.

Kriseova, Eda. *Vaclav Havel: The Authorized Biography.* Trans. Celeb Crain. New York: St. Martin's Press, 1993

Kristof, Nicolas D. and Sheryl WuDunn. *China Wakes: The Struggle for the Soul of a Rising Power.* New York: Vintage Books, 1995

Large, David Clay. *Between Two Fires: Europe's Path in the 1930s.* New York: W.W. Norton & Co., 1990.

Long, Huey. *Every Man a King: The Autobiography of Huey P. Long*. Cambridge, MA: Da Capo Press, 1933, 1996.

MacPherson, Myra. *All Governments Lie!: The Life and Times of Rebel Journalist I. F. Stone.* New York: Scribner, 2006.

Mandelbaum, Michael. *The Case for Goliath: How America Acts as the World's Government in the 21st Century*. New York: Public Affairs, 2005.

McCoy, Alfred W. *The Question of Torture: CIA Interrogation. From the Cold War to the War on Terror.* New York: Henry Holt and Company, 2006.

McDonald, Forrest. *Enough Wise Men: The Story of Our Constitution.* Richard B. Morris (ed.). New York: G.P. Putman's Sons, 1970.

Medvedev, Roy A. *Let History Judge: The Origins and Consequences of Stalinism*, Trans. Colleen Taylor. New York: Alfred A. Knopf, Inc., 1971.

Mill, John Stuart. *On Liberty*. David Spitz (ed.). New York: W.W. Norton and Co., 1975.

Miller, Barbara. *Guilt and Compliance in a Unified Germany: The Stasi Files Unveiled.* New Brunswick, NJ: Transaction Publishers, 2004.

Morgan, Ted. *Reds: McCarthyism in Twentieth-Century America.* New York: Random House, 2003.

Morris, Richard B. *Witnesses at the Creation: Hamilton, Madison, Jay and the Constitution.* New York: Plume, 1985.

Nash, Gary B. *The Unknown American Revolution: The Unruly Birth of Democracy and the Struggle to Create America.* New York: Viking Penguin, 2005.

Newman, Amy. *The Nuremberg Laws: Institutionalized Anti-Semitism.* San Diego, CA: Lucent Books, 1970.

Noakes, J., and G. Pridham, (eds). *Nazism: A History in Documents and Eyewitness Accounts, 1919–1945.* Volume I: The Nazi Party, State and Society. New York: Schocken Books, 1988.

Palmier, Jean-Michel. *Weimar in Exile: The Antifascist Emigration in Europe and America.* Translated by David Fernbach. London: Verso, 2006.

Paxton, Robert O., *The Anatomy of Fascism*, New York: Vintage Books, 2004.

Perkins, John. *Confessions of an Economic Hit Man.* New York: Plume, 2006.

Peterson, Merrill D. *Thomas Jefferson and the New Nation: A Biography*. New York: Oxford University Press, 1970.

Raskin, Marcus G., and A. Carl LeVan. *In Democracy's Shadow: The Secret World of National Security*. New York: Nation Books, 2005.

Rector, John L., *The History of Chile*, New York: Palgrave Macmillan, 2003.

Reeves, Thomas C. *The Life and Times of Joe McCarthy: A Biography*. New York: Stein and Day, 1982.

Reich, Wilhelm. *The Mass Psychology of Fascism.* New York: Penguin Books, 1970.

Reuth, Georg Ralf. *Goebbels.* Trans. Krishna Winston. New York: Harcourt Brace, 1990.

Rice Jr., Earle. *The Nuremberg Trails.* San Diego, CA: Lucent Books, 1997.

Rich, Frank, *The Greatest Story Ever Sold: The Decline and Fall of Truth From 9/11 to Katrina.* New York: The Penguin Press, 2006.

Roberts, Cokie. *Founding Mothers: The Women Who Raised Our Nation.* New York: William Morrow, 2004.

Robins, Robert S., and Jerrold M. Post, M.D. *Political Paranoia: The Psychopolitics of Hatred.* New Haven, CT: Yale University Press, 1997.

Roth, Joseph. *What I Saw: Reports from Berlin, 1920–1933.* Trans. Michael Hofmann. New York: W. W. Norton & Co., 1996.

Scahill, Jeremy. *The Rise of the World's Most Powerful Mercenary Army.* New York: Nation Books, 2007.

Schrecker, Ellen. *Many Are the Crimes: McCarthyism in America*. New York: Little, Brown, 1998.

Sheean, Vincent. *Not Peace But A Sword*. New York: Doubleday, Doran and Co., 1939.

Shirer, William L. *Berlin Diary: The Journal of a Foreign Correspondent 1934–1941*. Tess Press, 1941.

Shirer, William L. *The Rise and Fall of Adolf Hitler*. New York: Random House, 1961.

Solzhenitsyn, Aleksandr. *The Gulag Archipelago, 1918–1956: An Experiment in Literary Investigation, I-II*. Trans. Thomas P. Whitney. New York: Harper & Row, 1973.

Speer, Albert. *Inside the Third Reich: Memoirs*. Trans. Clara and Richard Winston. New York: Macmillan, 1970.

Stone, Geoffrey R. *War and Liberty: An American Dilemma, 1790 to the Present*. New York: W.W. Norton and Co., 2007.

Tucker, Robert C. *Stalin in Power: The Revolution from Above, 1928–1941*. New York: W.W. Norton & Co., 1990.

Vidal, Gore. *Dreaming War: Blood for Oil and the Cheney-Bush Junta*. New York: Nations Books, 2002.

Wollstonecraft, Mary. *A Vindication of the Rights of Woman*. London: Everyman's Library, 1929, 1985.

Zelikow, Philip, and Condoleezza Rice. *Germany Unified and Europe Transformed: A Study in Statecraft*. Cambridge, MA: Harvard University Press, 1995, 2002.

Zimbardo, Philips. *The Lucifer Effect*. New York: Random House, 2007.

Zinn, Howard. *A Power Governments Cannot Suppress*. San Francisco: City Lights Books, 2007.

Zinn, Howard. *Terrorism and War*. New York: Seven Stories

The American Freedom Campaign

Throughout history, Americans' faith in liberty and justice been tested, and we are living in such a time today. The American Freedom Campaign is a nonpartisan alliance of citizens aimed at restating nine basic American principles:

Fully restore the basic right to trial, habeas corpus, for everyone accused of a crime;

Prohibit torture and the use of secret evidence;

Prohibit the detention of American citizens as "enemy combatants" without proof of criminal activity on the president's say-so alone;

Prohibit the government from secretly breaking and entering our homes, tapping our phones or e-mail, or seizing our computers without a court order, on the president's say-so alone;

Prohibit the president from kidnapping, detaining, and torturing abroad;

Prohibit the executive from claiming "state secrets" to deny justice to victims of government misdeeds, and establish legislative-executive committees in the Congress to rule on the withholding of information on claims of "executive privilege" which obstruct Congressional oversight and an open government;

Challenge the constitutionality of signing statements, where the president seeks to disregard duly-enacted provisions of bills, by empowering the House and Senate to challenge them in court;

Prohibit military commissions except in places of active hostilities where a battlefield tribunal is necessary to obtain fresh testimony or prevent anarchy; and,

Amend the Espionage Act to permit journalists to report on classified national security matters without fear of prosecution.

For additional resources on what you can do as an individual and to learn more about the issues addressed in *End of America*, visit these websites:

American Freedom Campaign
www.americanfreedomcampaign.org

Chelsea Green Publishing
www.chelseagreen.com

American Civil Liberties Union
www.aclu.org

Human Rights Watch
www.hrw.org

The Center for Constitutional Rights
www.ccr-ny.org

The Pledge of the American Freedom Campaign

We are Americans. We do not torture, imprison people without charge or legal recourse, allow our phones and e-mails to be tapped without a court order, and above all we do not give any President unchecked power above the law and Constitution.

I pledge to fight to protect and defend the Constitution from the President's assault.

The Constitution protects American freedom. With checks and balances, and basic legal rights, it has prevented tyranny and safeguarded our liberty. Yet today, under the pretense of the "war on terror," the White House is dismantling the Constitution, concentrating power in the President, and undermining the rule of law.

I hereby join the American Freedom Campaign to educate my neighbors about the threat and urge my representatives to confront and correct these abuses of our America.

ABOUT NAOMI WOLF

Feminist, social critic, and political activist, Naomi Wolf raises awareness of the pervasive inequities that exist in politics and society and encourages people to take charge of their lives, voice their concerns, and enact change.

Wolf's landmark international bestseller, *The Beauty Myth,* challenged the cosmetics industry and the marketing of unrealistic standards of beauty, launching a new wave of feminism in the early 1990s. *The New York Times* called it one of the most important books of the 20th century.

Wolf's latest book, *The End of America: A Letter of Warning to a Young Patriot*, is an impassioned call to return to the aspirations and beliefs of the Founding Fathers. Wolf shows how events of the last six years parallel steps taken in the early years of the 20th century's worst dictatorships.

She is the author of, among other books, *Fire With Fire: The New Female Power* and *Promiscuities: The Secret Struggle For Womanhood.*

Wolf is co-founder of The Woodhull Institute for Ethical Leadership, an organization that teaches young women how to become leaders and agents of change in the 21st century.

A graduate of Yale and a former Rhodes Scholar, Wolf has written essays for *The New Republic, The Wall Street Journal, Glamour*, and *The New York Times.*